THE QUIRKY

WORLD OF PARKING

Four Decades of Observations,
One Parking Space at a Time

Larry J. Cohen, CAPP

ISBN: 979-87-09469-79-2 (Paperback)

DEDICATION

To Sarah, Nathan and Jacob for understanding that I chose a career in operations. Jobs in operations require you to be on-call 24/7/365. Rarely can you forget about work when you are home. And for moving up and down the Northeast and Mid-Atlantic in pursuit of advancing my career. This is a career that typically requires relocation to another city to advance upward.

To my employers, peers, and employees met along the way at Alber-Haff, Premier Parking, The University of Pennsylvania Health System, The Johns Hopkins Health System, Urbitran Associates, and The George Washington University. And finally, to the warm and welcoming community of Lancaster, Pennsylvania and the Lancaster Parking Authority.

TABLE OF CONTENTS

ACKNOWLEDGEMENTS

This book is not only for my parking peeps, but also for the public who often do not understand the job we do every day. My thanks to all those along the way, professional acquaintances, staff, friends, and even foes, who have inspired the many anecdotes I am about to share. I look forward to seeing you in-person soon.

To my brother-in-law, for his many edits to make my book the best it can be. After retiring from a career as a book editor, he was able to rekindle his skills to do a great job.

And to many of my peers who are discussed in the following stories. Names have been excluded to protect the innocent—and guilty! If you are angry with me, remember, it is about the story!

I even thank those who have shared their nasty interactions with me over the years. I am glad I found a positive use for them. It has been a rollercoaster ride; there have been so many amazing and crazy stories, yet also some tragic ones.

Life goes by so quickly and I always joked that each incident could go into a book one day—so here it is finally, albeit it took forty years.

As I have unfortunately experienced all too often in my career, my deepest thoughts go out to those with mental health issues who perceived committing suicide from a parking garage as their only path forward. This book is dedicated to you and your families as they try to find peace and meaning from such a terrible occurrence.

Larry J. Cohen, CAPP
February 2021

FOREWORD

"Innovative parking management practices and technologies play significant roles in urban planning and economic development, along with reducing congestion, encouraging turnover in retail districts, and support time-saving traffic flow. While parking is thought of as affecting the first and last mile of one's journey, there is also a human and emotional side that can elicit unexpected behavior. Larry shares his decades-long management expertise and his experiences with all the above attributes of parking, both of which offer a valuable service to our community of professionals. His book is a primer on parking interlaced with wonderful real-life stories and lessons."

Shawn Conrad, CAE

Chief Executive Officer, International Parking and Mobility Institute

"This is a book that needed to be written. Most of the public do not understand the day-to-day operations and the behind the scenes encounters that make up the parking world. Larry takes us on a journey through his 40 year career, from running his own business, to working in a variety of senior level positions at major hospitals and universities to consulting and most recently in heading Lancaster, Pennsylvania.

The next time you enter a parking garage, pay a meter, receive a parking ticket, or use a mobile app for parking payment, you will feel differently after having read the stories that he has put together in this must-read for our profession."

Mark A. Vergenes
President, Pennsylvania Parking Association, and
Former Chairman of the Board, Lancaster Parking Authority

PREFACE

The Road to the Parking Lot

While many of my friends had visions of a career in law, medicine, business, or teaching, I had no idea what my future would bring. I was a lost soul, more interested in playing sports and watching TV than studying for tests and planning a career.

As I stumbled about in my younger years in the early 1980's, contemplating what profession would take me through life, I came upon a job as a valet parking attendant at a company located down the street from my high school. As soon as I passed my driving test at sixteen years old, I was ready to go to work. With my license in hand, along with several friends, we were hired part-time to valet at restaurants, country clubs, private parties, and special events.

The job was great for a sixteen-year-old who was eager to see the world outside the neighborhood that he had spent most of his time growing up in. I drove nice cars at a variety of events, enjoyed seeing attractive women, sometimes received meals or fantastic leftovers, and gratuity (tip) money to spend while saving my paycheck, which I would use to purchase my own car one day.

Who would have known that more than four decades later, I would still be parking cars? Even my friends are amazed that I made a career out of the same part-time job that we all had in high school. But I am proud of and energized by the job I do every day and isn't that one of the most important things in life? Finding something you are passionate about and working in that field? People often tilt their heads like curious dogs when I tell them I work in parking. I am frequently asked, "Parking is a career? What the heck do you *do*?"

I reply that running a parking authority is like running many other businesses. One deals with personnel and finances, evaluates new technology, plans construction, and takes part in area economic development, to name but a few of my job highlights. Often the response is, "Wow!, I didn't know you were involved in so much!"

At the same time, some people do not care about anything a parking authority is involved in. They believe parking should always be free and rules never enforced, and our operation should be abolished.

A former Lancaster mayor told me on my first day on the job overseeing the parking in the city, "Never read the comments section of the paper in a story about parking. It will just divert your attention from doing your job." I agreed with him and told him I would not; but I must confess that I do peek at comments occasionally. As I will discuss later, public hatred can run deep at times.

This book covers my 40 years in the industry working in a variety of roles with many different types of customers, employees, and peers. I will share many of the serious, funny, crazy, and tragic events that I have experienced. All the stories are true. I hope they evoke many emotions along the way, and that by the final page you will have a better appreciation of the quirky world of parking.

Enjoy the journey!

CHAPTER ONE

THE BEGINNING OF A CAREER

After seven years of working my way through high school and college for a valet parking company, I decided to go into business for myself at 23 years old. I loved the company I worked for, they gave me an opportunity to advance, but I believed I could provide a better level of service. When I gave my resignation, I promised I would not take any of their existing accounts, even though I had no contract or separation agreement to abide by. I decided I would create my own niche business, I called it Premier Parking, and would base my company on providing a higher level of service, which included giving out long stem silk roses to all private function guests as shown on my first promotional postcard. *(Sorry for the yellowing card, it's 35 years old.)*

I took my life savings, around $3,000 and set up shop in the basement of my mother's house. In order to start the business, I had to pay a hefty deposit on insurance. The only company willing to insure a 23 year old with no experience in business was Lloyd's of London. Lloyd's is best known for insuring ships (including the Titanic) and insures high profile celebrities and other eccentric things. They more recently have insured Bruce Springsteen's voice and Dolly Parton's breasts (I kid you not).

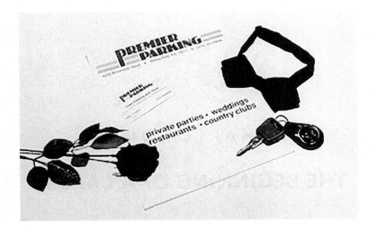

My business was successful from the start. I was fortunate to land major accounts, the most high-profile of which was the old Veterans Stadium in Philadelphia in the late 1980's. The stadium was the largest sports and entertainment venue in the region, so it was ironic that I was able to return to the stadium that in my younger years provided me my first real job.

I had a neighbor who was a security guard at the stadium. He would take me to the games and while he was working, I would watch the game with the grounds crew from behind home plate and hang around outside the locker room for autographs after the games while the stadium emptied. He eventually convinced me to start working, so I took the only job that would employ a 13-year-old. I sold programs. I walked throughout the stadium on hot summer days and nights with fifty pounds of magazines on my back. I can still recite barking out loud to the fans, "Hey programs, yearbooks, score cards and line ups." So, the irony did not pass me by as I now handled all events at the stadium, including Phillies baseball, Eagles football, and amazing big stadium concerts, including Paul McCartney and the Rolling Stones, all within my first year in business.

This account came to me when the Eagles had almost relocated, overnight, to Phoenix, Arizona, in an eerily similar scenario to the

Baltimore Colts actual move to Indianapolis, Indiana. When the owner of the Eagles at that time, Leonard Tose, was contemplating the move, Philadelphia agreed to build luxury boxes around the top of the stadium to generate additional revenue for the team. This was an ingenious idea given that those seats were by far the worst seats in the stadium. From there you could hardly see a player on the field, but you could watch the game on TV, use a private bathroom, and eat and drink as much catered food and beverages as you desired. Most importantly, you received free valet parking close by the stadium. That is how my company grew: with a mailed solicitation at just the right time!

The NFL Players Strike

During my time serving Veterans Stadium, there were many memorable games and concerts, but the most worrying time was the National Football League players strike in 1987. Our contract was with Eagles management and we were told to show up for work, regardless of the strike. I grew up in Philadelphia, so I knew the city was a strong pro-union town. But I did not realize how strong until I showed up on game day in support of my staff. Many of the NFL players boycotted the games, so teams hired replacement players or "scabs" as the unions referred to them.

I drove to the stadium, arriving very early, as my staff would usually do to get set up before fans showed up. I was told by my staff to park farther away than normal and walk to the stadium due to the potential altercations. Well, it did not take long to be recognized as someone heading to work because I was in uniform.

A nice gentleman with a big pole in his hand approached me and demanded, "Where are you going?" I replied that I was going to work. He said, "No you are not. Just get back in your car and drive home." Well, I did get back in my car, but I did not drive home.

My contract with the Eagles was on the line if Premier Parking did not work the game. Our contract could be terminated. I parked another half mile away and again walked to the stadium, avoiding everyone I could.

To my shock, people stood together, creating a human fence around the entire stadium, making it nearly impossible to enter. Luckily, by court order, the protesters had to provide a single pathway for fans and employees to enter and exit. The police stood by and watched in support of the union, so long as no one was seriously hurt.

As I passed through the line, many Eagles players were hand in hand with other union members. My goal was to keep my head down and get through the line as quickly as possible without being noticed. When I did look up, I was face to face with Eagles running back Keith Byers, one of their star players. He said, "Hey man, I know you! Don't you work for the Eagles?!" I did not like being called out as I was pushed through the line, but I was impressed that he recognized me from the various Eagles events I had attended. I cannot say it was a fun day; to the contrary, it was a very stressful day because each car entering the stadium for valet had its windows pounded on by picketers. Fortunately, the strike ended after 24 days and several home games, and parking procedures returned to normal.

We maintained Premier Parking for many baseball and football seasons, delivering white glove valet service to the wealthy clientele leasing the luxury boxes, all of whom demanded top notch service. While this account was our most important, many country clubs and high-end restaurants were also crucial to the success (and ultimate sale) of the business.

Liability costs, however, increased drastically through the years. Payment for accident claims, often for expensive cars, also with increased insurance premiums became staggering. After many years of vehicle accidents and claims, Lloyds of London eventually

priced me out of business. Luckily, I was able to sell the business in an all-cash deal, which turned into a very strange transaction.

As I moved onward to new opportunities, my office manager stayed with the company after I left. She called me one day, several years later, and asked, "Have you seen the front page of the Philadelphia Inquirer?" I had not. She told me that the gentleman who had purchased Premier Parking was on the front page of the paper and had been indicted in the Savings and Loan scandal.

I had always been curious and anxious about why the FBI contacted me after the sale of my business. I had paid all required taxes, so I knew it was not about me. But I was nervous and did not know what they were looking for. Luckily for me, the money used to purchase my business was not required to be forfeited. The gentleman who purchased my business was sent to federal prison and the business closed soon thereafter. His son did not have success taking over the business and within a year closed. No legacy business to look back upon, just a crazy story.

Transitioning

After I sold Premier Parking, many friends asked, "Why work for someone else?" Maybe I was too young or naïve to appreciate their question. But I was burned out at 28 years old, and most of my entrepreneurial juices had drained from my system.

Everyone sees the success, but not the stress and hard work that goes into owning your own business. Many small business owners will tell you they spend sleepless nights wondering how they are going to make payroll. I can attest to that. And when I could not make payroll, I was the one who didn't get paid that week. The increased insurance premium was my wake-up call that it was time to sell my business while I was ahead.

I decided to try out the corporate world. I came to grips with the fact I would have to work for someone else. Also, I knew that the success or failure in a job, in many cases, is based upon whom you end up working for. If the relationship with your boss is terrible, there is a high probability you will leave a job, even though you might have loved working at the place.

As I was contemplating the next move in my life, a good friend made me aware of a unique opportunity at a local major university hospital. The advertisement stated they were looking to hire someone to head up a new parking department. I felt my entrepreneurial background in parking would provide the perfect fit to build this new department. The hospital administrators stated that they felt the university was not fulfilling their parking needs adequately and that the hospital needed its own advocate. There seemed to be a line drawn down the middle of the street dividing the hospital and university. The university reaching decisions slowly and the hospital wanting their parking issues resolved quickly.

After eight hours of interviews with about sixteen people, I understood the dynamics and secured the job. If I were to get things accomplished, I was just hoping decisions would not involve that many people all the time!

The dynamics of having two parking directors within the same campus universe was awkward at first, but over time we found common ground. We worked together to resolve issues that affected the entire campus, not just the hospital on the one side and the university on the other side.

Learning the Ropes, Conferences and Comradery

Being a parking professional can be a lonely and isolating career at times. You do not have the immediate comradery that is often between professors, doctors, or lawyers. They are able to bounce ideas or problems off someone at their level who may be located right next door. When I worked at the university, professors were always conversing. At the hospital, physicians and administrators were also sharing ideas frequently. Although parking professionals can discuss many things with our staffs, sometimes you just want to talk with someone who is "walking in your shoes," someone dealing with the same types of issues you deal with daily.

Once I entered the university world, I felt the emphasis on enhancing my personal education. I began to search out and familiarize myself with the periodicals in my field. I found, not one, but three different magazines featuring parking issues; each magazine also sponsored a yearly conference. Yes, there are magazines and conferences about parking! And you learn more than how to park a car!

I had requested the opportunity to attend one of these conferences. I was thrilled that my employer would pay my expenses. To this day, I do not take these opportunities for granted. I am appreciative of all my employers who invested in me as I gained knowledge to benefit the program I was managing.

I attended my first national conference of the International Parking Institute in Atlanta in the mid-1990's. It was an eye-opening experience. I met others in this strange profession, with the same passion for parking! I felt as if I were starting a thesis on my way to becoming a Professor of Parking!

There were seminars on many subjects. Some were familiar to me and others I was eager to learn more about. Many presenters were authors of articles in the magazines I had been reading. The conference was the start of both networking with my peers and expanding my parking knowledge.

The best part of the conference, however, is the trade show. The first time I walked into an exhibit hall I felt I had landed in Parking Disneyland. I had goosebumps. Anything and everything parking related was on display. I could not wait to see new parking technology for revenue enhancements, examine garage designs and methods of repairs by architects and engineers, and even evaluate ways of ordering tickets and signs. Yes, I became an official Parking Geek!

You arrive back from a conference energized with new ideas to make your program better and feeling relief that you are dealing with the same type of issues as your peers. I have continued to attend state, regional, and national conferences throughout my career. Except as the years went on, my growing experience meant that I was also writing the articles and presenting topics to my peers. Does that make you an expert in your field? I think anyone who does the same thing for 40 years can claim to be some level of an expert. It is just nice to be able to "pay it forward," as the saying goes and share my experiences with newcomers who can benefit from learning.

Do not tell any of my employers, but I would have paid my own way if they had not paid for me to attend. I believe it is that valuable an experience and should not be missed.

If you cannot afford to attend a national conference, there are many great state and regional shows that are just as valuable a resource with networking opportunities to meet those in the profession from your area in a more intimate setting usually within a short drive.

Titles

Over the years, I have had several titles: Owner (better term, President), Coordinator of Parking, Manager of Parking, Director of Parking and Transportation, later switched to Director of Transportation and Parking to put more emphasis on transportation and transportation alternatives programs, Vice President of Parking Planning and Executive Director.

Over the same period, I have reported to an Executive Director, an Associate Vice President of Facilities, an Associate Vice President of Real Estate, a Vice President of Clinical Practices, an Associate Vice President of Architecture and Engineering, a Vice President of Corporate Security, Chairman of the Board, board members and a dotted line to Mayors.

Who Reports to Whom?

Although titles never meant much to me when I owned my own business, they are important in the collegiate world. For me, "Show me the money!" and the power to get things done is most important. Call me whatever you want, just make sure the paycheck does not bounce! Luckily, I have never had that happen.

When you are in operations, you do whatever you need to get the job done. Sometimes you must "take out the trash." But as your title changes, hopefully your pay and job responsibilities expand. Once I had proven myself by making sound staffing decisions, hiring the right contractors, putting customer service standards in contracts, enhanced ease of access by securing more parking areas and dealing with the cost of parking by setting up more discounted parking programs for patients, I was entrusted and able to take on new responsibilities and make decisions in the best interest of my employer.

Many organizations use outside survey companies to measure your job success. For example, Press Gainey is the most popular hospital patient satisfaction survey in the country. The results are held in high esteem, like television show ratings. If you do well in your area of responsibility in these scores, your credibility factor increases throughout the whole organization since it is a subjective measurement of many customers versus an objective measurement of the opinion of just your boss. Customer surveys can thus have a major impact on your career.

If you do well during in-house reviews and customer surveys, advancement opportunities may come your way, or you may be better positioned to seek a new opportunity elsewhere. The upward path of a parking professional does not always translate to advancement within one organization. But with your growth, change is constant for most of us throughout our career. You need to be prepared for shifting around from boss to boss, department to department, or even a new employer.

Sometimes, parking is like a bastard child that no one wants. Imagine sitting at an annual university strategic planning retreat with the goal of reorganization. I can imagine a senior administrator saying, "Okay, I'll take the police department, you take housekeeping, who gets parking?" NO! I don't want parking; way too many complaints about the cost and tickets!"

A new boss may not have had the experience of dealing with parking. Frankly, they may be shellshocked at the amount of parking complaints, whether it be the cost is too high or customers or patients receiving a parking ticket.

Unless parking is free, food service complaints are usually equal in dissatisfaction. Everyone can always complain about food. I have always felt empathy with food service managers.

As with any job, you must have a high degree of flexibility to deal with different types of bosses, each with different skill sets. In the parking profession particularly, someone with an advanced finance degree often will have a very different set of goals and style than someone from the police department. You must be adaptable to reporting to different types of individuals with different personalities.

In an ideal world, every boss should take the Meyers-Briggs personality test. The Meyers-Briggs is a widely used personality test. The results should be shared with their subordinates so each one knows how to best get along with them and is aware of their communication and management style which may be totally different than your previous boss!

90% Rule

People occasionally ask how I can do such an awful job like writing citations and making people pay for parking. I tell them 90% of what I do, I love. I have a passion for parking. I am involved in making decisions that affect the economic growth and vitality of the place where I work. Most days my job is very fulfilling and appreciated. The other 10% is awful. Mostly from interactions with angry, nasty customers. They are incensed over parking tickets, lack of parking, or the cost of parking.

But for any of us, there is usually 10% of our job that we dislike or would rather not do. So if 90% of our job is great, I think our career is a good one!

Leadership

I have read a book or two about leadership and attended many seminars. I live by the K.I.S.S. philosophy. Not the rock group (and my first concert), but the Keep It Simple, Stupid philosophy. Sometimes the best decisions are the easiest decisions. Do not make things too complicated. I am more a street-smart person than a book-smart person and rely on my basic decision-making processes. Gather the best information from your staff, review it, and then make a decision. If you need to pivot when the decision is not working out as planned, be willing to do so.

I also live by the early Boy Scout Law (honor), which I remember to this day. I was very far from ever being an Eagle Scout since I am not too much of an outdoorsman (mosquitoes love me too much), but still ingrained in me after all these years is, "a Scout is trustworthy, loyal, helpful, friendly, courteous, kind, obedient, cheerful, thrifty, brave, clean, and reverent." Words to live by in business and as a leader.

Many of you may have taken a *what type of manager are you?* test during your career. These tests show, in a general manner, how managing styles differ and how best to communicate, manage, and get along with others. My test results suggest that I am an outgoing Type A personality. I adapt well to the environment and circumstances I am placed within. I have been told I "play nice with others." Maybe that is why I can handle the politics of parking and deal with the many outside factors that influence our business in a positive or negative way, whether in response to public feedback or a developer in need of parking for a project.

For those of you interested in leadership, be your most honest self and lead by example, treat others how you would like to be treated, be straightforward, be honest no matter the outcome, and be loyal to those who are loyal to you.

These guiding principles of leadership have served me well over the years. Just as important is hiring competent fantastic individuals who can handle the day-to-day tasks and people who will do the job to the best of their ability. A true measure of success is how they react when the boss is not around. Will they relax or leave early when you are not in the office or use the opportunity to fix a problem or advance a new idea? Find those who strive to find a way to come to work versus finding ways not to work.

Many times, a leader's hardest job is dealing with the politics around your organization. Try to shield your employees from such distractions so they can do the best job they can. Your staff will appreciate this level of support immensely as part of your defined role.

I have always made it a point to make sure my staff feels appreciated. This can be shown in many ways, but I will always provide public recognition whenever possible, as I will discuss in the next chapter. Over the years, this has created a strong bond with my staff and a desire to follow me to my next career move.

You Get All the Credit and Take All the Blame

As a leader, you should never take all the credit for an accomplishment. It is rare that great things are accomplished by just one person. It is always best to share compliments amongst your staff, who support the work you get credit for.

At the same time, when things go wrong there is always enough blame to go around. It happens every day. The police are a perfect example of this. If an officer deals with a tragic situation, it is the police chief answering the questions. Or if a street is not plowed properly after a snowstorm, it is the mayor answering for it.

The same thing happens in parking. If one of my parking enforcement officers wrongly tickets someone, the complaints can easily end up on my desk. Is it your fault? Maybe through improper training, but no, you did not ultimately write the ticket. Good or bad, you are responsible for the entire organization or at least everyone under your command. You have the responsibility for not only your decisions and actions, but for everyone else who works under you.

When there is an issue, "no comment" does not work. You should show empathy and possibly remorse about what has happened, investigate the occurrence, and give a timely reply as to how the situation will be handled and resolved.

You Know Me

For a good leader, transparency with all staff is important. Make it a point to meet and talk with every employee. Sometimes the best ideas come from your staff.

No matter how much you have achieved in your career, however, on most days something brings you back down to earth with a bump. It is often a screaming customer. But on one occasion,

I was leading an all-employee meeting. As I made my way to the end of the three-hour agenda, I asked for questions.

A new employee raised her hand and asked *Who are you?* From then on, I always made it a point to introduce myself first before starting a meeting!

CHAPTER TWO

ACRONYMS AND ORGANIZATIONS

EGOT

Parking is a career for many individuals, but only a select few have achieved EGOT status in the field. What is EGOT status? An EGOT is someone who has won all four major entertainment awards: the Emmy, Grammy, Oscar, and Tony. Singer John Legend and Whoopi Goldberg, among others, have achieved EGOT status.

I was joking with a friend on his parking podcast (yes, there are parking podcasts!), that there should be an equivalent honor in the parking industry for someone who has worked in most, if not all, the different sectors of the profession. I have been a business owner, consultant, and parking administrator at a university, hospital, and city. The only thing missing on my resume is running an airport parking operation. An EGOT of parking, so to speak. The podcast host came up with an acronym: EMACU (Events, Municipality, Airport, Consultant and University).

My diverse experience allows me to share stories from many different sectors of the profession. Are you an EGOT or EMACU? Feel free to let me know!

APO

When I took over leadership of an independent municipal parking authority in Lancaster, Pennsylvania, in many ways it was the "Wild West of Parking." Many of the crazy stories I will share throughout the book are collected over the last ten years.

So many crazy things were happening, I could never have imagined that less than seven years later, the authority would earn the highest credential in our industry: an Accredited Parking Organization (APO). Yes, there is such a thing. The distinction is the apex of a climb for my organization. There is a list of over two hundred criteria that an organization must pass from A to Z to make sure you are running a "Best in Practice" program in order to be eligible. Criteria include human resources management, finances, operations, and public access, just to name a few. It was the culmination of years of hard work and getting the right people in the right positions. That hard work paid off.

To the public, APO provides credibility. It is the assurance that your organization is following "best practices" in every aspect of business. It is a benchmark of quality, which is important because a community may not know anything else about the business of parking other than we park cars and write tickets.

The APO award shows we can successfully operate on the same scale as organizations with much larger staffs and budgets. We are an organization that "adheres to a strict code of ethics and meets national and internationally endorsed standards for professionalism, accountability, responsibility, and performance."

An APO is an award and a commitment to ongoing evaluation and quality improvement. All parking organizations should strive for APO certification.

CAPP

After spending the early parts of my career in the hospital and university world, I realized that degrees and titles were important for a certain level of respect from your peers. Early on at the Hospital at the University of Pennsylvania, I was intimidated while working in high profile institutions with many Ivy League educated staff surrounding me. I was just a kid with a state university education. I felt I had to prove I belonged amongst my more highly educated peers. I always was cognizant to make sure my written and oral communications were at a high level. At the suggestion of my boss at the time, I even took a writing and speech class, although I did not believe it was warranted since I had proven myself successful in my communication and presented myself well amongst peers and superiors. Though they may have been more book smart, they were maybe not as street smart. So, I asked myself:

- Could I work towards a higher degree?

- Maybe a Master's degree?

- Something else?

I chose something else. My professional organization, the International Parking Institute at that time, had started offering an advanced certification program through the University of Virginia. A certification program in parking! Sounds crazy, of course! But what could be better for me? I enrolled and after two years, I achieved a Certified Administrator of Public Parking certification. The CPA or AIA of Parking, if you will.

It was a great personal achievement for someone who was not great at attending classes and taking tests. But what is the most satisfying part? Putting those letters after my name, and those I work with knowing I achieved something, even though they do not have any idea what the heck a CAPP is.

CPM

The National Parking Association offers a Certified Parking Manager program. It is geared toward entry and mid-level managers. It is a study guide-based test. It is a great program that can be completed in a relatively short period of time and provide the depth of knowledge needed for someone with future aspirations for a career path in the profession.

Professional Organizations

There is a trade association for everything, I know because I oversee the parking at a convention center. One week may bring a slew of pink Cadillacs for Mary Kay cosmetics, and the next week is a trial lawyer association. Parking is no different. Conferences and organizations are in place to support and advance each organization and to bring alike people to together to share experiences, thought, networking and ideas. The following are the main organizations for our industry.

- International Parking and Mobility Institute (IPMI). Majority of its members are consultants, architects, engineers, parking equipment and software providers and university, municipality, hospital, and airport operators.

- National Parking Association (NPA). Majority of its members are private property operators who run private garages and parking lots in cities around the country, airports, and stadiums, privatized municipal parking operations, vendors, and consultants.

Publications and Internet Sites

There are three major publications on parking. Each provides valuable articles on parking and transportation (mobility) issues. A variety of other topics are covered on a monthly basis and include such areas as lighting, electric vehicles, energy efficient infrastructure, design, construction, planning and marketing.

- *Parking and Mobility* is published by the International Parking and Mobility Institute.

- *Parking* is published by the National Parking Association.

- *Parking Today* is a publication from Parking Today Media.

- *Parking Network* is an international online network.

CHAPTER THREE

PARKING PERCEPTIONS

Parking 101

The term parking can be generally defined as *space in which vehicles can be parked*. Easy enough. Because there are so many different aspects of the business, however, stricter definitions exist within the different parking sectors.

As examples:

- For **hospitals**, parking means facilities with easy access for patients, visitors, and staff.

- For **airports**, parking means facilities for travelers to have easy access to the terminal. Airport parking also generates a significant amount of non-airport related revenue.

- For **universities**, parking means facilities for staff and students and coordinating other modes of transport, such as public transportation and biking. And with an emphasis on walking, carpooling and ride sharing.

- For **private operators**, parking means providing access to managed accounts such as office buildings, garages, airports, and stadiums. Valet parking is often provided.

- For **cities**, parking means on-street meter parking, parking enforcement, a Residential Permit Parking program, and street sweeping once or twice a month to keep blocks free of debris that could enter the sewers.

- For **businesses (vendors)**, parking means technology, access controls, accepting payments and creating statistics (metrics) for analysis in support of decisions in managing programs most effectively.

- For city **planners**, parking is about curbside management and accessibility, which is achieved through codes and regulations. They must manage the limited curb street space to provide parking and access for a variety of uses, including cars, bikes, pop-up parks, deliveries, taxis, and any other curbside needs.

- For **architects**, parking is designing structures that adapt to the environment. Garages should no longer look like a large concrete monolithic structure.

- For **engineers**, parking is putting the building blocks together to create a facility that is structurally sound and built to last for many years.

- And for the **public,** parking should be simple, easily accessed, close to their destination, and inexpensive.

Why should parking be paid versus free for public use? This is a question I have been asked many times in my career, and I will provide an answer later in the chapter.

Can You Avoid Paying a Parking Ticket?

Let us deal with this burning question right up front. The simple answer is sometimes yes and sometimes no. It usually depends on what state and city you are fighting your case in. Parking citations are either civil or criminal. Civil means if the citation is not paid, it may go to a collection agency or the city or state may use other methods to seek payment, including a boot immobilizer on the car or towing it to an impound lot if you have a certain number of unpaid tickets or are parked in a towaway zone.

In our jurisdiction of Lancaster, parking citations are a criminal offense, so after you receive a citation you typically have 30 days to pay before it is sent to a district justice that covers the area the citation was written in. We send out a notification at 15 days that your payment is due within 30 days. If you want a hearing in order to plead not guilty, you are notified that you must attend your case on a certain date and time. The affiant, the police officer or parking enforcement officer who wrote the ticket, must also attend to defend his actions. If the affiant does not attend the hearing, the judge will usually rule in the defendant's favor and you will not have to pay the ticket. You can decide how much your time is worth to attend court based on the price of the ticket. If your vehicle was also towed, the costs probably are enough to take the chance. In many cases, you can negotiate with the affiant before the case is heard in the court. You may be able to get certain fees waived or dismissed as part of a settlement of your outstanding citation(s). You do not need legal representation to fight a parking ticket, but I would suggest an attorney if the citation is criminal.

Convenient, Inexpensive and Plentiful

Figure 1 is several years old, but I believe is still valid. It basically suggests that in a vibrant city, parking can be convenient, inexpensive, and plentiful. It suggests you can have two of the three choices but rarely all three. Is that true for your town, city, or university? Do you agree?

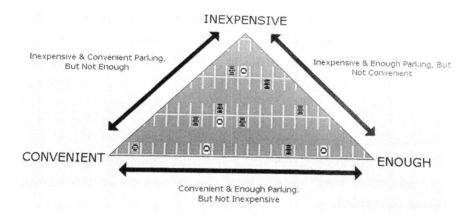

Figure 1

First and Last Impressions

Many times, parking is the first and last impression someone has of your city, airport, university, business, or hospital. So, it is important to make sure the first and last impression is a good one, regardless of whether you can provide inexpensive, convenient, and enough parking in just the right space for the visitor.

Parking is Just Space, Right?

Parking is just space, right? So why pay for it?

Because parking garages and flat surface lots cost a significant amount of money. The land needs to be acquired and the garage or spaces designed, built, maintained, cleaned, and staffed.

Believe it or not, in most parts of the United States, a garage parking space usually costs between $10,000 to $100,000 per space to build, depending upon variables such as location, complexities of the project, and cost of land. Thus, an average small parking facility with 300 spaces could cost $3 million to $30 million!

In a flat surface parking lot, the cost can be between $3,000 to $20,000 per space. Costs attributed to drainage, paving, lighting, landscaping, and perhaps fencing. The cost for a 300-space surface lot could run between $900,000 to $6 million, and this may or may not include buying the land!

But how about on-street space in a city? Shouldn't that be free?

If you said, "Yes," then maybe the following two stories will change your mind.

A Board Game Controversy

Even board games can create a controversy when it comes to free parking. Donald Shoup, professor of urban planning at the University of California, Los Angeles (UCLA) and author of *The High Cost of Free Parking*, states that the free parking square on the board game Monopoly risks reinforcing misconceptions in players from an early age about the true cost of parking.

He suggests that the world-famous board game do away with its Free Parking square. He argues that on-street parking, in effect, gives away for free some of the most valuable land in a city.

Monopoly's Free Parking space should be renamed Paid Parking to encourage a more realistic attitude to parking costs.

Shoup adds that the one thing in the game that does not add up is that the probability of landing on Free Parking is the same as landing on Go to Jail. Most children do not go to jail when they grow up, but almost all of them will park free when they get real cars because parking is free for 99% of all automobile trips in the United States.

Shoup accepts that no one wants to pay for parking but insists that cities should not be planned around free parking. Parking costs do not go away just because the driver does not pay. Expenses shift into higher prices for other city services; thus even people who cannot afford a car pay indirectly for free parking.

He says the United States now has more parking space per car (at least 900 square feet) than housing space per person (about 800 square feet)!

He concludes that all the free parking greatly increases the amount of driving, which congests traffic, pollutes the air, and contributes to global warming.

As you will see in the following case study, paid and managed parking is an extremely important aspect of a community.

A Case Study for Paid Parking

When thinking about the importance of paid parking, I found this example to be very poignant.

Given the option of having a downtown shopping area with paid or free parking, most people would naturally choose free parking. In fact, introducing paid parking has been a continual struggle between municipalities and citizens, with municipalities often protesting paid parking and many business owners claiming that it hurts business.

Most folks in Galveston, Texas would have agreed. But it took a powerful force of nature to change their minds. In September 2008, Hurricane Ike hit the city, devastating many of the municipality's homes and businesses.

The downtown district was one of the most heavily affected; even all its parking meters were destroyed. It took more than six months just to clean debris from the streets. As businesses dug themselves out of the rubble, they began to open again in hopes of rebuilding financially. Unfortunately, the physical reconstruction of the city brought with it a parking-related problem: on-street parking was being monopolized by contractor and employee vehicles, leaving business customers and patrons with nowhere to park.

The parking meters had previously ensured a systematic rotation of vehicles, but the monopolized parking spaces were proving detrimental to the growth and revitalization of the city's business district.

Many businesses futilely attempted to control parking on their own using signs but the community soon realized that if they were ever going to truly rebuild businesses, restoring order to downtown parking was imperative. Though the city acknowledged the importance of re-establishing a parking management system, it obviously needed to prioritize other aspects of the revitalization.

Business owners, therefore, took things into their own hands and formed a committee on re-establishing a parking system. In talking with citizens and other business owners they were able to establish criteria for a new parking system, including a user-friendly system that accepts multiple forms of payment, has the ability to run on solar power for energy efficiency, and provides multi-space parking meters that do not clutter the streetscape.

Galveston's parking system today provides residents and visitors with the convenience of paying with bills, coins, credit cards, and even their phone. The income generated from parking goes right back into the parking system to support program upgrades and additional parking spaces as needed.

Prior to the hurricane, Galveston's downtown business owners would never have wanted paid parking let alone advocated for it. They took parking for granted until it was gone. Since they have re-instated paid parking, the flow of traffic has normalized and customers have returned. Throughout the rebuilding process, re-establishing paid parking was a major milestone in returning Galveston to normalcy.

"The Perfect Storm of Parking Enforcement."

Have you ever received a parking ticket (also called a citation)? Or has your car been towed?
Have you ever been extremely upset about it?
Have you sworn never to visit that city or town again because of the ticket?

Receiving a parking ticket results in all types of reactions. I usually see someone get the most upset when they have paid the meter, but the time *just* expired as they are returning to the vehicle. They arrive in time to find a parking enforcement officer (PEO), or as they were called years ago, meter maid, ticketing the car. (Not sure what they called men – meter men?) If you did not know any better, you would think they were hiding in the bushes waiting for the meter to expire. Is it a conspiracy theory?

The actuality is that most PEO's are on a walking or driving route and are not aware of how much time is left on a meter until they are in proximity. But the perception is that this is a planned attack. In most cases, this is not true.

If it is planned, then the PEO would be standing and waiting for the payment to expire. The PEO should not be conducting business in this manner, nor should their supervisor be training them in this manner. Parking enforcement should be conducted as outlined and approved by City Council in city ordinances.

City ordinances are the laws that govern a city. There are also ordinances that specifically deal with streets and traffic that may include broader issues of sign changes or additions and traffic lights. There are rules, policies, and procedures at other organizations that define parking rules. Some institute a grace period to allow for leeway in enforcement and how much expired time should pass before someone gets a ticket.

A grace period may create a "moving scale of expired time" when the time is considered expired. As an example, your monthly parking bill is due on the first of each month, but you have a grace period to pay by the tenth. If your payment is received on the eleventh, it is then considered late, and you are charged a late fee. Sometimes a customer will complain that they are only one day late or one minute, when they are really 11 days or 11 minutes late!

The point is, when providing a grace period, you are late at the end of the time that is considered expired. Customers need to understand that a parking violation, whether one minute or 11 minutes with a grace period, is then expired.

Some cities have addressed this issue by providing a button for a free 10 minutes of parking or by programming a grace period into the enforcement software. It is up to each city, city council, and their ordinances for on street enforcement to agree upon what the city desires in their enforcement rules.

Chalking

Chalking is the enforcement procedure for marking parked cars on a tire to make sure the vehicle is not parked in the same space for over the maximum time designated on the sign on the block where the vehicle is parked. When the PEO arrives back to the block after the maximum time limit, the chalk mark indicates that the vehicle has not moved. Vehicles used to be chalked with actual chalk on a stick to make sure the car was not parked longer than the time limits posted. If so, a parking citation is then issued.

But recent rulings in several states have stated that actual physical chalking of a car tire is considered vandalism, and the practice has had to cease. For enforcement in the twenty-first century, chalking is done virtually. A picture of the tire and position of the tire stem is pictured in the enforcement software on handheld units. If the vehicle has not moved after the noted time on the sign, the picture of the tire and tire stem will be at the same position as it was when the picture was taken.

Envision a tire as a clock. The tire stem will be in position as a hand on a clock. For example, when the car is parked, the tire stem is at 3 p.m. When the PEO returns, if the tire stem is still at 3 p.m., there is a high probability that the vehicle did not leave the parking space and the owner is given a parking ticket.

Quotas

Quotas is the term used to describe the practice of making sure PEOs write a certain number of tickets per shift or enforcement area. Driven in part by increasing budget demands, this has been a practice that sheds negative light on the profession. There could be incentives involved for the PEOs or management to write more tickets, and competition between PEOs with rewards.

I have always discouraged this practice because I believe in the true meaning of parking enforcement; it is a policy to make sure the community is adhering to the ordinances that were developed for governing the use and turnover of parking spots for the benefit of the community given that there is a limited amount of on-street parking.

My benchmark has always been to provide enforcement at a level that if the public were to question how often we enforce a block, the public cannot question the fairness and frequency. In a ten-hour enforcement period, we typically cover each block no more than four times per shift. That is four passes through each block over a ten-hour shift. That is adequate enforcement to make sure that everyone adheres to the rules and pays for parking.

Frequency of Enforcement

Each city or university with any level of a sophisticated parking management enforcement system (<u>not</u> including old-fashioned hand-written police tickets!) should be able to tell you how often parking enforcement passes through each block in a city or campus. The handheld units are mini-computers or mobile phones encased and programmed to identify cars parked, meters paid or expired, and can print and issue tickets. They are either connected to a cloud-based system with no physical hardware in the office or a computer in an office that downloads the enforcement tickets into the parking system for payment. A good enforcement system will allow you to be able to pay a ticket online or in an office right after a ticket is issued.

Frequency for enforcement can range from "never enforcing" to every 5 to 10 minutes.

A popular shopping area in my city claimed that we were over enforcing the block. Once we pulled our historical data, we showed them that we were enforcing each block three to four times per day over the course of ten hours of paid parking hours. That seemed reasonable to them, and the perception of over enforcement became a moot issue.

It is crucial to communicate with the business community to make sure there is transparency in how a parking program conducts its business. There should be a partnership between businesses and the parking authority to make sure that on-street parking space is turning over at a reasonable rate. Customers should be able to find a parking space near the business they want to visit. The parking authority and business community should both want the same outcome.

Parking Myths

The way we think about parking entrenches many perceptions that are simply not true.

Perceptions can be reality. Perceptions should be accordingly addressed with facts.

The following myths are several of my favorites in relation to parking within a city.

Myth #1 "Successful cities have plenty of parking"

- Surrounding towns may have more free parking, but no great city is known for its cheap, abundant parking.

Myth #2 "It's difficult to find parking in cities"

- Customers are not interested in how many parking spaces there are in the city. What matters is how easily someone can find a parking space.

- It is best for cities to free up parking spaces using common parking strategies:

  1) Time limits to create turnover

  2) Demand-based pricing with lower parking rates in less used areas and higher prices in higher demand areas

  3) Pricing that makes convenient on-street spaces more expensive than long-term parking in garages

- It is important to combat perceptions of parking shortages. Often, people complain of parking shortages when actual car counts show that only 75% of on-street spaces are occupied at any one time. The best way to combat these perceptions is in the same manner as dealing with the perception of over enforcement. Provide data to support the reality of the situation. If there is an actual parking shortage, the data will confirm it.

Myth #3 "Parking needs to be right outside the front door of a business"

- In most situations, there is no reason why most business customers cannot park a block or two away from the front door of a shop. In comparison, at a mall people will park half a mile away if the building or store is within "line of sight." In a city, it is thought that you must be parked on the block of the business. In a thriving downtown area, individuals should enjoy a couple block walk and visit other stores along the way!

Customer Satisfaction

Two of my favorite bumper stickers collected over the years have the saying, "Parking Should be a Non-Event" and "Parking Should Be Friendly, Not Free." These two slogans have provided a guiding principle for my career.

"Parking Should Be a Non-Event"

Parking should be a non-event. Isn't this what those in the parking business should be trying to achieve every day? Our paying customers want a parking experience that they do not have to think about. Drive to places of work, leisure, or shopping, and park easily for the least amount of money possible.

Afterwards, pull away from the parking space and head home or elsewhere. Parking as a non-event should be the goal of parking operators around the country. If parking were always a non-event, our customer satisfaction scores would be through the roof every year!

"Parking Should Be Friendly, Not Free"

Parking should be friendly, not free. There actually is a desire to provide friendly customer interactions, but parking is not like buying a meal at a restaurant or taking a trip. No one wants to pay for parking, and no one wants to pay a parking citation!

Providing service that is perceived as friendly by customers, requires an added level of understanding as to how they can best be treated.

As a parking operator and/or owner, the goal should be to provide pleasant service when we encounter our customers.

Friendly, however, does not mean free?
Is food free in a restaurant?
Is gas free for your car?

Parking is a business, with many expenses, and the goal is to have enough parking to serve the needs of the community. Without sufficient income, readily available parking would not be plentiful and the impact on businesses may be dire. Justified or not, some businesses may blame a lack of parking for their business failure. In a parking authority that is a true non-profit, all income goes right back into the program to create more parking, enhance technology to ease payment, and upkeep existing space and infrastructure.

Parking professionals should explain that what we do is a business with many costs and that the desired outcome is to provide safe, clean, and accessible parking.

Why Drive? Who Needs Parking Anyway?

For many areas in our country, where there is no available form of public transportation, driving is a necessity. A case can be made for maximizing the use of alternative forms of transportation, instead of driving and then parking. Parking, public transportation and alternative transportation modes now fall under a singular term, mobility. Mobility is the mode of transportation that gets you to and from your destination.

Critical in our discussion of mobility, is the "first and last mile". How do we best serve the public in getting them to and from work without the need for additional parking? The most critical need to address is the individual's first mile after leaving home and the last mile when arriving at work. This is where the future of transportation (mobility) lies if the goal is to reduce the need for parking. Transportation Network Companies (TNC's) like Uber and Lyft play a critical role from the private sector in handling this current demand. How will the public sector react and pivot into the future to handle this demand? Will it continue to be handled by the private sector?

Public transportation in a 40-passenger bus cannot give you personalized service and cater to each individual, but micro-transportation (mobility) can. Micro-mobility is identifying similar paths to work for similar riders during the same time frame. Think of a car or van pool for public transportation. More smaller vehicles with more specific routes in the future will result in less parking demand for single occupancy vehicles (SOV). The success of catering to individual transportation needs will help to support the need for less parking in the future.

Parking Minimums

There are still cities that require parking minimums for each new development project. For each new square footage of office space or hotel room, a parking space is required. For example, in many hotel brand agreements, each hotel room needs the equivalent of one parking space. If the developer cannot provide the one-to-one hotel room to parking space ratio, the brand will not sign off on an agreement.

I can tell you that more than once, a developer has come to my office and would not leave until I signed off on a letter guaranteeing to provide one parking space for each hotel room that was being built. Yes, sometimes multi-million dollar development projects hinge on parking!

But over time, cities have started to eliminate the parking minimum requirements to enhance economic growth. In many cases, developers do not want to use their valuable capital dollars to build parking. They want to use their money to build buildings. The public sector as well is reluctant to use capital dollars to build more parking.

With less emphasis on creating new parking, there has been a shift to transportation alternatives and the use of micro-mobility TNC's such as Uber and Lyft. Universities have often led the way in creative transportation modes outside of parking. Biking, electric bikes (e-bikes), walking, scooters, carpools, vanpools, incentives to ride public transportation, living close to work, are all valid programs to cut down on individual vehicle dependency. The use of financial incentives or special accommodations like locker rooms for bike riders to change, bike storage facilities, closer parking for carpooling, and lower parking fees for carpooling are enhancements and incentives to not drive and to use other modes of transportation.

Many universities have signed off on the Climate Action Plan to reduce their carbon footprint on campus. A plan for carbon emission reduction over the next 10 to 15 years will include reducing the number of vehicles arriving on campus. Therefore, it is imperative for these schools to seek reduction in single occupancy vehicles (SOV's) arriving on campus and to provide incentives and a level of convenience for employees and staff to give up driving alone to work.

Perhaps self-driving electric cars will be the mode of the future to get everyone to work. New automobile technology keeps evolving and will be discussed along with the future of parking technology in my next chapter.

CHAPTER FOUR

PARKING IN THE 21ST CENTURY

The first parking garage was built in 1918, as part of a hotel in Chicago. The first parking meter, called the Park O Meter, was used in Oklahoma City in 1935. These facts always seems to come up in games like Jeopardy. Now you know.

In its first 85 years of existence, paid on-street parking was dominated by coin operated meters. How often did you have to plan your day knowing that you would need a pocket full of quarters or other coins for feeding the parking meter? (In the early days it was a penny, inflation!)

How lucky did you feel when pulling up to an old-fashioned meter and found time remaining on it? It was like winning the parking lottery!

Alas, winning the parking lottery is becoming more difficult with advances in technology. In the United States, most parking innovation has occurred during the last fifteen to twenty years. There have been significant changes to the on-street parking experience during this time that has served as a customer service enhancement for payment options and a method to maximize on street revenues.

Those New-Fangled Parking Machines

Multi-space meters (kiosks) were used in Europe for many years before arriving in the United States. They provided an opportunity for planners to declutter the streetscapes and surface parking lots of urban cities and universities while providing additional payment options in addition to longstanding coin payments. The opportunity to pay for parking with bills and credit cards were an added feature which delighted the consumer. In addition, each unit is able to cover anywhere from several parking spaces to an entire block or surface lot.

A segment of the population was not happy with the new meters. Some people were so upset that they even shied away from street parking because they did not want to learn how to use the "new-fangled" meter.

I spent many hours over the past ten years guiding mostly older customers through the transaction process. One lady covered her eyes and screamed, "I don't want to learn this!" You would have thought I was going to steal her purse. Some people, not only senior citizens, do not want to learn anything new; they just want return to the old ways. "I will carry my pocket full of quarters and be happy about it," they chant. A similar analogy is using a computer; some will eagerly embrace it while others will not.

In the early years of the kiosk, some cities used a pay and display method. After you paid, the meter issued a ticket which you then displayed on your dashboard.

The other method was to pay by space, which required numbering each space on the street or lot so that the customer could pay at the kiosk and input the space number.

The evolution of these methods has led to pay by license plate. In the age of tracking everything with one consistent identifier, the license plate number is input into the machine. It is not an easy task at first to remember your license plate, but after doing it several times it becomes easier. You can take a picture with your cell phone rather than try to remember it. But from a parking operator's perspective, the new kiosks provided an opportunity to maximize on-street revenues. Even using your license plate, you are still able to pay for parking using all the various payment methods.

Probably the biggest financial benefit to the organization is unused time that is not credited to the next driver, as it is with a single old-fashioned meter. No longer do we experience the excitement of winning the parking lottery. The opportunity to "piggyback" unused parking payment is becoming a thing of the past. But with that lost opportunity is the availability of many different payment options.

Credit Card Meters

By dividing an old-fashioned meter in half and adding a new sophisticated credit card unit to the top, you know have a credit card payment option. This ingenious invention spread rapidly throughout the country, especially in the manufacturer's home base in California and in particular Los Angeles. The new meters in the latter came with unintended free marketing since they are visible in commercials, movies, and TV shows filmed in the City of Angels.

Mobile Phone Payments

Mobile phone payments have only been in existence since the early 2000's. The advent of paying for parking using a mobile app has been a win-win scenario for consumers and parking operators.

Using a mobile app for payment of parking has provided for many benefits. Most important are:

- Eliminated the need to carry coins.

- Drastically reduced the propensity of an individual getting a parking ticket since it allows the individual to add more time from anywhere.

Your lunch meeting is running late?

No problem, you can go into your app and add time to the meter.

You have lost track of time?

No problem, the app will alert you via your selected advance time notification how much longer you have until the meter expires.

Buying a new car in the future?

There is a good chance that you can pay for parking from your car.

The downside?

There is a user fee, typically in the 25 to 35 cent range, for your transaction. Not many people complain about the fee since it is better to pay a small fee than receiving a $10 to $75 parking citation. That alone should convince you to get a mobile payment app on your phone.

User acceptance of this technology is incredibly successful. For example, Washington, DC, has one of the highest user percentages of mobile app meters in the country. They encompass more than

85% of on-street transactions in some parts of the city. Even in other cities, mobile app payments typically account for 25% to 50% of on-street transactions.

Mobile phone payments have also solidified a major goal of on-street parking operations: compliance over enforcement. We should want our customers to pay for parking versus receiving a citation. Any city worried about the decrease in citation revenue should know it will probably be offset by the increase in meter revenue. Many individuals who might not have paid for parking because they did not have coins may be inclined to now pay using the app.

Other benefits exist for the organization, including the reduction in back office finance and accounting time spent counting and reconciling coins due to less time collecting coins on the streets.

The Future of Mobile Apps

Given my expertise in parking, I created a list of my desires for the future of mobile apps. The most relevant are:

- Advertising and promotions with local merchants. It would be like Waze navigation with pop-up ads when parking. For example, an ad could say, "While you are parked on our block, stop in for 10% off a cup of coffee."

- Mobile apps would be used for all parking transactions, on street and in garages. Maybe they could even include tolls at some point. Like a toll pass for parking. Some car manufacturers are already including this in their car app platforms.

- Instead of many different parking app companies, one app does it all. The major apps are already available through Apple and Google.

- With increased use of parking apps, there are no capital costs for on street hardware. It allows for the reduction in spending on single and multi-space kiosks, thus keeping costs down that would typically get passed along to the customer.

There is an abundance of new and exciting parking apps available in the marketplace today and many more are being developed. I would love to list them all, but as an example, I am just listing the ones that I currently have on my phone.

Parkmobile

One of the major companies that offers on street mobile parking payment.

PayByPhone

Their name is almost the generic name for on street mobile app parking payment, like tissues and Kleenex, but another good on street parking provider.

Spot Hero

Spot Hero is an app that allows you to compare prices in an area where you are going to park. It shows the best rates and allows you to book the space. I have used the app in New York City many times, and it has saved me lots of money.

Prked

Prked allows someone to post parking available on their private property. Maybe you have a yard or driveway that you can lease out for a ballgame or concert. Here is a place to make the connection.

The Impact of Autonomous and Electric Vehicles (EV's)

First, I must confess, I own a Tesla. They are a technology company building cars. Tesla is currently the dominant electric and self-driving vehicle in the marketplace, though the other major car manufacturers are working to catch up. An EV Hummer, Mustang and Cadillac is coming soon. Even Apple may end up being the biggest challenger in the electric autonomous vehicle market.

A basic autonomous vehicle is taking cruise control to the next level by allowing old fashioned cruise control to now allow the changing of speeds to stay within a safe distance in between cars in traffic. Fully autonomous is most easily defined as vehicles that have the capability of driving without the need of driver interaction. Fully autonomous vehicles can drive, stop, and change lanes without the assistance of the driver. This is already available in many Tesla's today. With Tesla selling 500,000 units in 2020, the EV's and technology are here to stay.

There will be other electric vehicles forthcoming, with each manufacturer providing a certain level of autonomous self-driving capabilities. Not all electric vehicles will have advanced self-driving features, but it does seem to be the way of the future. From a parking perspective:

Will autonomous vehicles need a place to park?
How will this technology affect parking demand?

A Tesla can already drive and navigate without you stepping on either pedal. Tesla taxis are already on the streets of New York City and other pilot cities and will take riders to their destination with minimal driver involvement.

But a self-driving vehicle will either need to park at some point or be in constant movement all day. The vehicle could either perpetually pick up and drop off other riders, but most likely it will have to return to its place of origin, or park in a lot or garage while the owner is at work or shopping. Eventually, a self-driving autonomous vehicle will have to park somewhere.

How will autonomous vehicles affect the design and use of parking spaces?

If the vehicle parks itself in a garage, does the garage need to provide the current drive lanes and width of a parking space to open and close doors? It does not *if* the entire parking lot or garage is used for EV's only. Currently, with less than 5% of vehicles in the autonomous category of car sales, we are still years away from the time when a parking garage would be for self-parking cars exclusively, although a taxi lot with 100% of self-driving cars requiring less parking could happen sooner.

Mandates from California and other states to follow will require only non-gas powered vehicles to be manufactured by 2035. With the shifting away from gas-powered vehicles, part of the role of parking operations will be to provide EV charging stations or areas for this expanding market. Depending upon the state, tax credits and grants are available to provide the infrastructure needed for the charging stations. In the future, charging areas may not require the station. Vehicles may just need to drive on top of a charging pad or area, like wireless charging for a smart phone that is plugged in to a charging station versus just placing your phone on a wireless mat to charge. Further evolution in battery technology will allow for mobile charging packs you can keep in the vehicle.

Parking operations should be amenable to providing EV charging units. They can be provided as a courtesy or a fee-based structure can be adapted as an added revenue source. By providing this value-added service whether for free or a fee, there will eventually be an increase in the demand for these parking spaces.

I have put charging stations in all our garages, and I have been told on more than one occasion that customers have chosen our garages because we offer charging. Maybe it just makes good business sense, especially when I visit your city. I will be in my blue Tesla.

CHAPTER FIVE

THE POLITICS OF PARKING

"Do I Fix Parking Tickets?"

Many times throughout my career overseeing on-street parking operations, I have been asked by friends, family, peers, or acquaintances, "I got a parking ticket (for whatever reason). Can you make it go away?" The answer is a resounding, No. I do not void tickets. I have survived in this business a long time by doing the right thing. Can you imagine if I were to void a ticket for a family member or friend, and the public became aware of it? That would not be good.

"What is the worst thing that can happen?" they ask. In many situations, the outcome could be a potential loss of job, which I have dealt with on occasion because an employee did not do the right thing. I have always lived by the motto, "Do the right thing." That is, making the correct decisions in fairness to everyone and not making decisions that will benefit myself or those I know.

I have a friend who always complained that parking enforcement never passed through his block. Now that the authority oversees the area, enforcement comes by his block at least several times a day. And at least once a month he gets a ticket, and he pays it knowing I do not fix tickets. A good friend does not put you in the awkward position to say, "No, I cannot fix your parking ticket."

Democrats and Republicans

Through the years, I have supported Democratic and Republican candidates. I have benefited from being neutral and not having my political affiliation affect my career. Sometimes political affiliation is an issue in parking operations, and many times it is a non-issue. But I know some peers, however, who have lost their job based on political affiliation.

I tell a story later in the book about being a finalist for a job and maybe part of the reason I was not chosen was not being the right party. But my goal in public life has been to do my job, regardless of political affiliation and ruling party.

Let Others Help You Do Your Job

It is always a battle to implement new parking rates or extend enforcement hours. Look for those opportunities where you do not have to make a case alone, but with the help of others.

There was no on-street enforcement on Saturdays when I arrived at the authority. Not surprisingly, the streets were clogged with employees parking all day and not allowing customers to use these vital spaces. The merchant community led the charge to City Council to have Saturdays enforced. City Council was a lot more sympathetic to the request of the business community than if the request came from the parking authority. It is nice that the business community is well educated and understands the impact on their businesses when there is not enough on-street turnover of spaces. It is even better when others make the sales pitch for you for increased enforcement.

Parking as an Incentive for Recruitment

Parking can be a very emotional and divisive issue, specifically at places like universities and hospitals, or basically everywhere. Parking plays a larger role and impact on the hierarchy of an institution than you might expect. I frequently think about the quote that says, "You know who is important by where they park every day."

Many highly recruited professionals have mandated a reserved parking space next to or as close as possible to their place of work. Sometimes they even have their parking space included as part of their compensation package. Sometimes recruits may or may not accept an offer based on parking and they may take a job elsewhere. I know this has happened because I have been a part of these decisions.

There can even be negotiations regarding a reserved parking space sign, with the name of the individual on it, such as, "Reserved Parking for Dr. Smith Only." I have always advised to not put someone's name on a reserved space. Everyone will see it, and if they are not a fan of the individual, they may take it out on the car parked in that space with some level of vandalism. When I present that premise, I can usually persuade the requestor not to have his name on the reserved parking sign.

It helps from a parking management perspective not to have to monitor and enforce a reserved space. Additionally, a reserved space is taken out of use for other times of the week since it always needs to be kept open for that one person.

Halting Development Projects – It Only Takes One

It can be said that the development of a parking garage can sometimes be "a great unifier of public dissent." A new garage can be a common "enemy" that can unite a community if it is believed that the impact of the project will have a negative effect on a neighbor, a block, or the entire area.

All development projects face tough questions as they go through the approval process. That process may include a historical commission (maintaining the integrity of historic property), shade tree commission (yes, a commission to review trees to be lost) and the land development process, which brings together all agreements, easements, and other aspects of a project for final permission to start building.

But the question arises, *"Can't we find a better use for the land than a parking lot or garage?"*

I was developing a garage extension on our surface lot that was zoned accordingly (city designation on how land can be developed and for what types of uses) that would alleviate new parking demand for our convention center. The goal was to not develop along city streets, but to build any new parking behind already developed projects along the street, which this garage expansion project achieved.

Yet the power of one individual, and social outreach, was able to stop the project dead in its tracks despite all its merits of supporting economic development. In the presence of a governing board, like city council, decisions can be made with or without merit, based upon great influence by their constituents.

We had completed the design for the new garage expansion. We spent over a quarter million dollars in design fees, and all it took were several neighbors stating that their property would back up to the garage and would be visible from their backyard to stop it. They even brought in their children to state it would affect them if they were looking at a parking garage while playing in the yard. Whether the children's statements were scripted by the parents or not, that was enough to bring an entire project to its end.

It is called due process, and I am not going to defend whether the project should have been terminated or not. My point is that building new parking can unite citizens in opposition, and they often have a sympathetic ear in city council or other governing bodies. Many times, the value of new parking garages is not appreciated for the economic benefit it can provide.

The same can be said when new parking meters are proposed on a city street. The power of a community, or even just the residents on that block can sway the decision of city council members. These are their constituents, and whenever a large group of citizens shows up at a public meeting, council members will take notice.

This is not a desired outcome for someone who manages and tries to expand parking to meet demand, but the merits of due process are to be respected.

Developers

I have dealt with many developers over the years. I am respectful of their business acumen and admire how they build their wealth in support of the growth and development of communities. Some developers, however, always have their hands out looking for free, i.e., taxpayers money to support their own business growth. Some developers can take advantage of the public decision makers. Bad decisions between developers and city administrations can hamper a city for many years, including selling or leasing private assets that include parking lots and garages. There is no better example than the City of Chicago that I will discuss later in the book.

Admire developers, respect them, but beware of their own occasional self-fulfilling motivations of building personal wealth on public dollars.

Lawsuits and Settlements

It should always be a goal when working with contractors, vendors, and developers to do your best to avoid litigation and lawsuits. Usually, no one wins a lawsuit except the lawyers. It is always best to try to settle your differences. My rule of thumb is a settlement should be painful for both sides. If that is the case, you have probably met in the middle for a successful settlement.

I Hate Building Parking Garages

No one believes me, but I do not want to build parking facilities. Yes, they are fun to design, but the cost of the debt will impact your operation for the next 20+ years. The public may think that those of us who run parking programs are adamant about wanting to build new parking structures, when the answer is the opposite. The total expense to construct and build any new building is ridiculously high, while putting an organization into a position of paying off a lot of debt. If solutions can be implemented without building structured parking, then it is best to exhaust these options first. A good operational assessment of how current parking is being utilized may uncover ways to alleviate demand, at least in the short-term.

A sampling of questions to ask:

> *Will long term demand for parking warrant the capital costs?*
>
> *Is there adequate projected cash flow to pay for a new garage for the next twenty years?*

And as part of a good operational assessment:

> *Are current garages designed and striped to maximize use of space?*
>
> *Can "overselling" spaces, like hotels and airlines, alleviate overall demand?*
>
> *How is the current parking location being used between daily and monthly parking?*
>
> *Are any vehicles parked or stored overnight that reduce available space?*
>
> *Is the proper rate structure in place to create turnover?*

For example, many garages can be re-striped to add 10% of new space to a garage. It is better to exhaust all operational changes that can be made before taking on the costs and going through the approval process for a new garage. Part of that process are the politics for approvals that will be discussed in the next chapter.

CHAPTER SIX

CITY HIERARCHY

Parking administrators report to many different types of bosses. It can be a one-to-one relationship within a city department, or a city parking authority with a relationship to a board of directors with five to seven members that are appointed by the mayor. Most board members serve either a set term or serve "at the pleasure" of the mayor; meaning the mayor has the right to ask for their resignation, or can remove them at any time. Mayors will want a board in place that has the same vision, hopefully in supporting the economic growth and development of the city versus generating additional revenues to support city expenses.

Depending on the city's financial situation, the mayor may also request a payment from the authority or services in lieu of payment in supporting city initiatives.

If the mayor and a board member do not see eye to eye, the board member may be asked to resign. In some cases, a board may be replaced in its entirety from mayor to mayor. That is within the mayor's rights if there is a differing of philosophies in how the board should conduct its business. It happens many times with a change of administration. Just as a new President of the United States appoints their own cabinet. You may or may not agree, but the mayor is the ultimate boss.

City Council

Besides the mayor, many big decisions require the approval of city council members. In our city, the ordinance (rules and regulations governing the city, including parking) for adding parking meters or increasing on-street meter parking rates must get the approval of city council. City council members are swayed to vote in the best interest in the community they serve. So, making decisions to increase any parking rates is usually a hot topic and major political issue. When city council's constituents voice concerns or complaints, members will listen, and act as warranted. The challenge is convincing the board, mayor, and city council, and the public of the need for parking changes that can include rates or added meter spaces.

For example, I had proposed a meter expansion plan in Lancaster to add meters to ten new blocks in the central business district. The process went smoothly and was approved by council. One of the blocks was next to a subsidized housing tower. The housing complex has limited parking on their surface lot and made significant use of the on-street parking for care takers and visitors. When they got word of the approval and subsequent installation of meters in that block, the residents filled a bus and attended the next city council meeting. If you cannot figure out how this story ends, my folks were on the streets the following day removing all the parking meters they had just installed.

Mayors

I have been lucky to be able to transition smoothly from one mayor to another and to have had a great relationship with both during my ten years in my current position. They both are respectful of the job I do daily and of the overall operation of the authority. Thankfully, neither meddled in my day-to-day operations.

But I cannot say the same of other cities I have encountered. In one instance, a mayor from another city demanded the authority hire one of his old high school friends. Since they had no other choice, the authority hired the individual. The only issue was that he had just been released from prison and had to have an ankle bracelet so probation could monitor his whereabouts. He was not what I would call the ideal candidate, but sometimes mayors abuse their power to influence decisions. Luckily, my mayors have never put me in the position of hiring someone I would never hire on my own.

The first mayor I worked for directly had a favorite saying regarding parking:

"I get complaints all the time that you are either ticketing too much or not enough. You can never win when it comes to parking."

Luckily, he understood parking is a no-win situation.

I started my public career working for my first mayor during my first seven years on the job and was fortunate to be able to transition to my second mayor and stay in good standing over the past three years. With both, I have had good mutual trusting relationships. The motto being, *"I will watch your back if you watch mine."*

But many of my peers do not share the same fortunate fate. Many cities and towns still live by patronage. Friends of politicians and/or large donors to their campaigns are often taken care of after a successful election.

For the parking program, what happens is that an unqualified person is hired who does not have the job skills to handle a complex multi-million dollar operation. They usually fail miserably, putting the authority in poor financial condition to the detriment of the entire community. The painful lesson is obvious: Hire competent people!

Dirty Politics

It is always wise to try to keep parking out of the political process. I have talked about municipalities (luckily, not mine!), being forced to hire unqualified individuals and mayors meddling in daily operations, but the reality is I have dealt with the politics of parking in all my jobs throughout my career.

When I started writing this portion about dirty politics, my wife said to me, "maybe it would be a good idea to wait until you retire to write your book." I compromised, and for this section alone, I will wait until <u>after</u> I retire to tell some of these crazy stories in Version 2!

CHAPTER SEVEN

MORE POLITICS

When Not to Raise Rates

If you are running a city parking operation and have a mayor to report to, I would suggest not raising parking rates during an election year. It is not the time a mayor will appreciate the focus on parking.

Some candidates for mayor or other political office do tackle parking as an agenda item. I am not the first to hear a candidate say, *"If elected, I will abolish the Parking Authority and make parking free for everyone!"* While this is a good sound bite, once someone is elected to office and he or she learns why parking fees and enforcement are vital to the economic growth and vitality of the community, he or she usually softens his stance.

Fundraisers

Another personal rule of mine is to never attend political events, unless perhaps for the incumbent mayor. The one time I did attend a political event (which a friend persuaded me to go to), I was cognizant of staying in the background and not being seen. I was just enjoying some hors d'oeuvres and a drink and casually talking with some people I knew. So how did this come back to haunt me? Well, a newspaper photographer took a picture of the candidate. I also was in the picture standing far in the back but recognizable. This picture ended up on the front page of the city paper.

The next day the mayor said to me, *"What the heck were you doing at that fundraiser? I saw you in the picture."* He was half joking, but that was the last political event I have attended. Just in case.

Voter Suppression?

An attorney contacted me and threatened to file a lawsuit stating that the authority was guilty of voter suppression. I was shocked by these comments.

We work with the local board of elections every year to block off parking spaces so constituents in the city have easy access to their voting location. We had done this for many years without any issues.

In 2020, however, his client claimed she had received a parking ticket because she parked far outside the voting area and could not figure out how to use the multi-space parking meter. So she decided not to pay at all. Well, she received a ticket and blamed the complexity in paying for parking as a deterrent to voting. This was the first time I found that requiring parking payment could be a voter suppression issue!

CHAPTER EIGHT

PARKING CARS AND SAVING LIVES

I was watching a local political debate on television. The odds that suicides from a parking garage would come up in such a discussion were about 1000:1. But that is exactly what happened. A candidate stated that mental health issues need to be a priority, otherwise *"people might start jumping off parking garages."* I was very surprised to hear it in a local political debate. I have experienced these sad and shocking events too many times in my career.

Saving Lives

We have hosted many memorable events in our garages; weddings, photo shoots, and car shows. And in the summer, some not so endorsed events such as naked sunbathing on the roof. Yet in our public parking facilities, sometimes there are emergency situations that can occur, even life-threatening ones. Based on our experiences and an in the interest of being proactive, we began an initiative to put all our training together and prepare our staff to handle all types of emergencies.

Saving lives is the umbrella term I use that includes awareness and staff training to help prepare for and equip my organization to deal with all types of emergencies. It includes not only traditional first aid and cardiopulmonary resuscitation (CPR) training, but also the installation and training in automated external defibrillators (AEDs), and mental health and QPR (question, persuade, and refer) suicide prevention. All staff, including myself, are trained in all these areas.

While some of this training is traditionally required by all individuals who regularly work or deal with the public, the mental health component is not as common.

A few years ago, I became a reluctant expert and the go-to person on garage suicide mitigation strategies. We were experiencing a rash of suicides from our largest parking garage, which is the highest open-air facility in the city. The garage became a kind of iconic site for those who were pondering suicide. In a two-year period, there were five successful suicides.

I decided an aggressive, proactive game plan was needed. I brought together a cross section of community members, including mental health experts, police, legal and others to discuss what could be done to eliminate these tragic situations.

First, we decided to keep people off the roof unless they were there to park their vehicle. We established a zero-tolerance policy for the rooftop of the garage. Following city guidelines, we posted No Trespassing signs so we could enforce keeping pedestrians off the roof.

We made a commitment to do something, although we could not fence off all levels. We added chain-link fencing to the top two-levels of the eight-story garage. This was expensive, but worth it to make those levels off-limits. Other physical barriers can be added such as trees or landscaping to help provide a deterrent to jumping since those attempting suicide want a clear path below.

We also began patrolling the area. We park our cars at the top levels for extra monitoring. Security uses bike patrols to ride through the garage.

The community group decided to work in support of suicide prevention. We posted suicide prevention posters that included a local number to call for help. We also instituted suicide prevention training, using a course called QPR, as referred above, so we could be ready if we found a person considering suicide. This training encourages talking with the individual until the appropriate authorities arrive such as police, fire rescue, or mental health counselors. We also recognized the need to provide professional assistance to staff who may have been involved with a suicide situation or had seen a dead body.

I am proud to say that since our QPR training, our staff has talked down some potential suicides, and there have been no other deaths by suicide in this garage.

Suicides are still much too common. Roughly 50% of my peers have dealt with an attempted or successful suicide. According to recent data from the Centers for Disease Control (CDC), nearly 45,000 people in the United States lost their lives to suicide in a most recent year. More than 54% did not have a known mental health condition. In almost every state suicide rates increased from 1999 to 2016. The CDC encourages communities to have programs in place to support those with suicidal thoughts.

Preventing suicide is just one way our authority is working to save lives. We have installed AED's in all our garages and facilities. They are public places, and we want to be able to provide immediate assistance to someone who suffers a sudden cardiac attack. It could be the difference between life and death. The AEDs have audio instructions in both English and Spanish to help attach the device properly and administer electrical shocks, if needed.

As mentioned previously, all our staff are trained and certified in CPR and first aid. We went one step further and added training on mental health first aid. We also offered in-house training on substance use disorders, including opioids. In a world with multiple stressors and time constraints, we believe it only makes sense to provide mental health training to our staff. Mental health training, along with the other courses, aid employees, their families, and friends, and the community.

Saving lives is a priority in our organization. Training staff to be prepared for almost anything they could encounter in their work with the public ensures that we are helpful, confident, and efficient. I encourage all parking organizations to consider providing comprehensive training to their staff. You could save a life.

Caveat: Be prepared for any potential legal action. In the legal world, you are damned if you do anything, and damned if you don't do anything. Nonetheless, I suggest you take some level of action to correct a pattern of incidents from the same structure. Media response can also be either supportive or sensationalistic. Be careful how you discuss suicide attempts and encourage reporters to avoid descriptions or headlines that increase the risk, and instead focus on helpful resources in the community.

I could never have imagined that I would be using my experiences in dealing with garage suicides to support institutions nationally to assist in conducting mitigation assessments and putting strategies in place to support the effort. If these efforts save just one live, it is worth it.

CHAPTER NINE

PUT ON THE B.R.A.K.E.S.

Like many millennials, my son did not see a need to drive if mom or dad could drive him around. But with an impending full-time summer job, he needed to get his driver's license.

My driver's training with him was very strenuous. Many times ending with screaming and yelling, especially when he hit a mailbox along the road. Overall, it was not a very good experience for either of us.

I knew there had to be a better way for him to learn to be a good driver. I needed to relax, and my son needed more confidence and advanced driving experience, more than a typical driving school would offer.

I wanted to find a program that teaches new drivers how to deal with emergency situations. I did research and found a program based in North Carolina. B.R.A.K.E.S. stands for Be Responsible And Keep Everyone Safe. Its mission is to prevent injuries and save lives by training and educating teenage drivers and their parents about the importance of safe and responsible driving. B.R.A.K.E.S. was created by drag car racer Doug Herbert after the tragic deaths of his sons in a car accident.

Some of the driver training includes collision avoidance using selected road courses to teach elevated steering control; a distraction exercise to teach increased focus and concentration; a wheel drop-off recovery exercise to teach the proper method of retaining control when the vehicle drops a wheel off a highway shoulder; a panic stop exercise to give teenagers safer and more controlled responses when braking in an emergency; and a car control and recovery exercise that teaches the skills necessary to maintain or regain control in wet or icy road conditions.

After learning about the program, I knew this was right for my son and that it was taught by the right people. Luckily, the program was coming to my area and, as you learn when you attend the class with your child, the program is as much for the parents as it is for the kids. Overconfident or timid kids are brought into balance after going through this program. And parents are humbled by the process. The "behind the wheel" experiences and simulations with trained professionals are first class.

After a three-hour morning program, I was so impressed that I wondered if my experience in parking could help B.R.A.K.E.S. in any way. After a conversation with the founders, they were thrilled that my contacts could help them find large parking lots around the country to run the program. They were expanding their program and sought stadium size parking lots that could handle the multiple courses needed for training. They were able to contact many stadium lot operators, and now they are training more of our kids to be safe and proactive in their responses to a variety of different driving scenarios.

Whether the training is with B.R.A.K.E.S. or a similar program, I highly recommend your child's participation. In fact, I do not just recommend this program for anyone new to driving, I would require it.

CHAPTER TEN

PRESIDENTIAL PARKING, HOW PARKING WAS HANDLED FOR A PRESIDENTIAL INAUGURATION

The George Washington University is located just four blocks down Pennsylvania Avenue from the White House. The campus community is accustomed to a variety of disruptions that can occur from presidential motorcades and dignitaries passing through campus.

When it comes to "emergency planning," leadership has been ahead of the curve in dealing with potential emergency situations, whether they be weather related or potential terrorist activities. During my time at the university, we would drill, drill, drill for real life situations to test *contingency* (how to deal with the issue) and *continuity* (how to maintain operations) preparedness plans.

The level of security under normal conditions is that parking garages are not only equipped with card access and cameras at entry/exits, but with roll down gates. So when the university undertook the task of planning for the predicted largest turnout expected in presidential inauguration history for Barack Obama, we tackled the issue head on, and planning was underway just after the election results in late fall 2008.

Our meetings quickly outlined the obvious parking and transportation questions:

- Is there adequate parking to accommodate all our needs?

- When and if we run out of parking, what will happen?

- Will shuttles buses be able to access campus and route stops?

- Will staff be able to get to and from work?

The campus was in the "soft" perimeter (allowing movement within the "hard" perimeter) of the inauguration and located at the end of the parade route. Several months beforehand we were told by the Secret Service and other law enforcement agencies that those unaffiliated with the university would not be permitted within the perimeter on Inauguration Day.

It was to be a four-day event; with a concert featuring Bruce Springsteen, Beyoncé, and others in front of the Lincoln Memorial Sunday night (also just several blocks from campus), Martin Luther King Day (declared a National Service Day), the Inauguration, the Inaugural Parade, and Inaugural Balls Monday night (we are the only university that has an Inaugural Ball).

Over 1500 outside guests were registered to stay overnight on campus (students were not permitted to rent their dorm rooms but could apply for overnight guest accommodations) most were arriving on the Friday and Saturday prior to Inauguration, which would provide us the opportunity to know in advance whether our parking capacity levels would be sufficient for Inauguration Day.

Hotels were also in high demand from Richmond, Virginia as far north as Wilmington, Delaware, over two hours north of D.C. At that time there was a concern about overflow occupancy in the residence halls and visiting students arriving last minute that may decide to sleep in their vehicle if they could not have access to the dorms. But this did not become an issue.

We were in close contact with our affiliated hospital, which decided to have only essential personnel on campus on those days. The Inauguration is also a university holiday (good for those who did not have to work), thus further lessening the parking demand on campus and helping in the planning for the anticipated 2.4 million visitors coming to town.

We will not get into a debate about the size of the inaugural ceremony attendance, but, in comparison, the George W. Bush inauguration had an estimated 400,000 visitors. Estimates showed that the Mall could handle 1.5 million from end to end. The remaining visitors would overflow right into the campus. Although the number of people that came to watch was large, they did not reach the projected numbers and thus our campus boundaries were clear.

Part of our back up plan was that in case we ran out of parking, we would reach out to private operators in the vicinity. The Kennedy Center for Performing Arts has a large garage, and we had a written agreement that we would be able to rely on one another for space as needed. The Kennedy Center had *The Oprah Show* and a free Aretha Franklin concert on Martin Luther King Day, but nothing planned for Inauguration Day, which would allow us to use their space.

Headlines across the country leading up to the inauguration put the fear in everyone that an "Inauguration Overload" was imminent for all parking and transportation resources within the city. The Metro subway system is extensive and (although not fully appreciated by the locals) it is the best in the country for handling the number of people we anticipated would make their way into the city. Lines to enter and exit the Metro system snaked for several city blocks just to enter the stations. Parking congestions to enter the Metro parking garages and lots also caused backups on highways, as noted by the local traffic reporters. It became apparent that one of our biggest concerns would be pedestrian traffic from the campus Metro stop to the Mall. The street disruptions were massive, from the Virginia side. Almost all bridges from Virginia to DC closed for an extended period.

Essential personnel figured that they could take the Metro, walk, or bike to campus, but the 15 to 20 degree temperature curtailed those plans. Therefore, many essential personnel prepared to sleep over Monday night since the odds of getting onto campus on Inauguration Day seemed bleak. Over 200 essential personnel including facilities staff, university police and parking staff either slept on an air mattress in an office (not too bad), available residence hall space, or army cots set up in the basketball arena.

Staying overnight proved beneficial. Some attendees of an inaugural brunch on campus, which started at 8:00 a.m., started arriving at 6:00 a.m. to beat the traffic. We were able to quickly send someone over to open the garage.

As the day turned out, most visitors relied on public transportation (with very, very long lines). Since access into the city was blocked and/or detoured, university shuttle buses were able to run with altered stops outside of the perimeter, and the staff that were needed either stayed overnight or came to work prior to 4:00 a.m.

The National Guard provided a safe perimeter to campus and if you did not have a proper ID card or a specially designed ID card for visitors, you were not able to drive onto campus. Mostly, there was an ongoing sea of pedestrian traffic from 4:00 a.m. throughout the day and night.

As with most major events, planning was key. Someone commented to me that planning for the Inauguration was like planning for Y2K (remember that?); a lot of planning but not much of an issue. That was fine with me. This monumental event left a lasting impression on everyone involved.

CHAPTER ELEVEN

THE BUSINESS OF PARKING

Most people would not believe that Parking is a $100 billion a year industry. There are many different aspects to the business. I cannot cover them all, but in this chapter I will try to cover many areas that you may or may not be aware of.

A Mission Statement to Support Business

I believe every organization needs a mission statement that is easy to memorize and can be shared with the public. My authority statement is simple but defines a broader vision and why there is an organization that oversees all aspects of parking. Our mission is *"to support the livability, growth and development of the city for the benefit of residents, businesses, and visitors."* It is not controversial, which is a win in the public eye.

My Life as a Full-Time Parking Consultant
(But Now Part-Time!)

From a business perspective, I will discuss my time as a full-time parking consultant working for a private engineering firm over 20 years ago. Even though my glimpse behind the scenes was a short one, it gave me valuable insight into this side of the business that has helped me in dealing with consultants.

For those in day-to-day parking operations who have envisioned sharing your years of experience and telling novices how to run their operation without doing it yourself, then consulting may be for you.

On the other hand, your opinion may differ, or at least give you the perspective to seriously weigh the pros and cons of a career in parking consulting. For those who think the grass is greener on "the other side" (referred as "the dark side"), you should weigh the options and evaluate the main job responsibilities you would assume as a consultant.

I had always envisioned life as a full-time consultant. Cut to daydreaming sequence. Traveling the world, evaluating parking needs, providing recommendations, and then moving onto the next project without having to worry about the implementation. Sounds like the ideal job for someone accustomed to the rigors of day-to-day operations, right? But as a fellow consultant told me, "It's not the glamorous life it appears to be." He was right. Sometimes you have to find out for yourself.

I spent one year as a full-time parking consultant. Nowadays, I conduct part-time consulting on my days off on the side, or as they say, my "side hustle." As I embarked on my temporary career shift to a consultant, four major job responsibilities came to the forefront: 1) sales/marketing, 2) proposal writing, 3) "teaming" with other firms, and 4) study work. Right away you will find out there is not enough time in the day to balance these varied and demanding job responsibilities. I will discuss each of the areas of responsibility below.

Marketing and Selling

As the business mantra goes, "you are only as good as the business you bring to the firm." No matter what else you are doing on the job, you are always selling the services of the company. Selling should be easy but it really isn't. For those not accustomed to cold call sales, this can be a daunting, demoralizing task and the toughest aspect of consulting. Everything from cold calling people in the news, to contacting parking acquaintances/friends in your address book is fair game. The ones who get back to you can be considered friends.

Friends and past business acquaintances do not always translate to good business opportunities for a variety of reasons. Although they may want to provide you business, there is the timing of the new projects to consider, bidding processes in place that may or may not have a low-bid criteria, political insiders who are awarded work regardless of their level of experience, steering business towards political financial contributors, or just better qualified and experienced firms.

The reality of the role hit home at a meeting with an established authority director, when he said to me, "I always meet with salespeople..." Thanks, but then again—*ugh*. Remember, operations folks are used to being chased rather than doing the chasing. It has always been the best to be the end user. I also realized that the vice president title bestowed upon me does not really mean too much in the outside world.

A sale is all about building long-term relationships. The company you work for must be willing to invest the time, money, and support of the profession to make this happen. If your firm seeks immedi-ate gratification, they are doomed to fail. The business approach in consulting cannot be compared to selling a used car. This is not a quick one-time sale. It is building a long-term relationship and part-nership to support the growth of those clients you serve.

Proposals

Proposals are a written plan with the price for services for consideration for a project that a potential client would like accom-plished. Many potential clients put out a request for proposal (RFP) to different firms to submit their ideas for consideration. You can spend many hours answering written proposals that may or may not be awarded to your firm. Sometimes this is demoralizing, depending upon the amount of time and effort put forth to try and win the business. You may have plenty of time to submit a response to the proposal or you may have only several days.

- For someone who prefers to have their schedule organized and planned out - fuhgeddaboudit!

- For someone who does not like to rush at the last minute to take care of things - fuhgeddaboudit!

A proposal arrives and the rush is on to get it done. Written by the deadline. Build a team with other experts by the deadline. In the mail by the deadline. Arrive by the deadline. It is a constant frantic pace to meet deadlines, and once you finish and take a deep breath—the next proposal arrives. And the process starts all over again. It never ends!

The unfulfilling part is that you can spend day upon day, hour upon hour, and not get the business. If you are lucky enough to be "short listed" (one of the finalists) with the opportunity to present your proposal in person, your odds of getting the job are better, but still not guaranteed.

It is an extremely competitive business which keeps prices in-line with other equally qualified firms.

Pick a Team

Whether they tell you so or not, not all consulting firms can be everything to everyone. This is where "teaming" comes into place. The goal is to form a team of consultants who can provide all the services you need for a particular project. For example, will the project need local representation to enhance the chances of winning the bid? Fine, we will team with a local firm to provide one of the myriad of services required on a project. Will we need a firm to provide traffic studies? Fine, we will team with a traffic study firm that has done work for the potential client in the past. Do you need minority participation? Fine, we will seek out a minority participation partner. (This should be done whether required or not.)

I was not fully aware of the extent of teaming, but it is a very common practice with almost all projects bid and awarded. In a strange business twist, the lead firm is in essence becoming a partner on a project (that can be multi-millions of dollars) with a firm they may or may not have even met or worked with in the past. Somehow, it seems to work out, although now I understand how communication breakdowns occur. When you have two or more distinct firms working and billing costs on the same project, there can be breakdowns on evolving and ever-changing projects.

Studies and Designs

Studies are reports that give professional opinions based on facts to resolve an issue. If we believe we need a new parking garage, we can commission a study to analyze data, talk with key stakeholders, hold public meetings, and so on. The study will give us facts based on current demand and project future demand based on those facts.

The designs are usually done by an architect to provide renderings of different ideas of how a project can look upon completion based on input from the owner. A conceptual design can be done in the proposal process. The actual design will happen once you secure the business.

Congratulations, you "win" one (the term for being awarded a job)! No time to celebrate, though, since you must get to work. But this is the most fulfilling part, where your parking knowledge and experience count. Architects and engineers are experts in their field. Remember, however, it is <u>you</u> who will operate the facility for the next 20 to 30 years! Your input with an operations background should count just as much as those designing the project. You need to make sure your voice is heard!

The study work can be very fulfilling if you are a very detailed person. There is nothing as satisfying as solving the parking problems of a client based on your years of experience dealing with the same type of issues. It is ironic that no matter what operation you encounter, we deal with many of the same types of problems.

The Fork in The Road

Twenty years ago, I decided I did not have the passion to be a full-time consultant. Although I found a great deal of satisfaction in solving parking problems for clients, all the work in getting the business just did not fit my personality. I yearned to be back in day-to-day operations and leading a team.

In hindsight, I feel good that I will not look back upon my career and say, "I wish I had given it a try." I am lucky that I settled back into the operational world and can also provide consulting services on a part-time basis to clients who seek me out (on my time off from work). My goal was to make you aware of the pros and cons. I certainly have a better appreciation for all the consultants who serve our profession every day.

The Personal Touch

I was overseeing a request for a proposal to manage one of the garages in our portfolio of properties. We were down to two finalists.

The first finalist talked about how large a company they had become, how many employees they employ, what their growth in revenue plan was expected over the next several years and pro-vided detailed spreadsheets to prove it.

The second finalist came in with nothing in hand, sat down and basically said, *"I will take care of you and your customers as if they were part of my own family."*

The second finalist won the contract. The moral of this story is to provide the highest level of customer service possible and treat your client as if they are the only one in the world. No need to razzle and dazzle someone to show your growth when all they really care about is how well you will take care of them.

References

A company I decided to conduct business with was relatively small compared to other companies I was looking to hire. When

I asked the owner for references, she stated, "There is no need to provide you just several references that I pick – of course they would be the ones to give you a good reference. I want you to feel free to call any or all our clients. They should all provide a glowing recommendation of our services. If not, please let me know."

Based on that response, I knew I was going to hire this company. They stood behind their word, not just with some clients they conducted business with, but with all their clients. Providing the highest level of service to all her clients paid off. The business is very successful and has achieved tremendous growth.

CHAPTER TWELVE

MAKING MONEY IN PARKING

"All Good Parking Lots Turn Into Buildings One Day"

Another one of my favorite sayings is, "All good parking lots turn into buildings one day." Typically in a growing urban environment, entrepreneurs with vision will acquire land, turn the land into surface parking to generate cash flow, and eventually may sell the land or partner in its development. The property will almost certainly become more valuable as developable land than as a parking lot. A developer wins in buying or leasing the land, maintaining cash flow while the land appreciates in value to the point it becomes more valuable to develop. A true win-win for those looking to build a real estate portfolio starting with parking lots.

On the public side, the other common scenario is development on a university campus. The use of surface parking lots is a placeholder until the next big donation dictates building the next research center.

Daily Rate Variations

The operator assesses each specific facility to ascertain how to best maximize revenues and create an effective pricing strategy based on the facility location and who uses it daily. Some garages in competitive areas may offer a daily "early bird" special rate for those who enter and depart a facility by a certain time.

Another strategy is to provide a "teaser" first half hour or hour rate and increase the hourly rate quickly to get to the maximum rate per day. This may be achieved through three hourly rates, the first hour, the second hour, then the maximum rate.

As a municipality, we provide an hour by hour fee throughout the day. Hourly rates are for each hour up to ten hours to achieve the daily maximum rate. But rates can also be set to change parking patterns.

Changes in parking behavior can be achieved through a passive rate structure. For example, if the goal of the facility is to not have all day parking, then you set an all-day rate that is cost prohibitive and parkers will eventually seek other options. You are not telling a potential customer to not use your facility, but you are setting the rate to discourage all day parking. For example, this may occur in a prime hospital patient facility that employees will use on occasion. Instead of a confrontation between an attendant and employee at the entrance of the garage, let the rates dictate user patterns and the impact of available inventory and revenue.

"Lost" Ticket

The lost ticket rate should be the daily maximum price. No one parking for a day will pretend to lose a ticket to pay the maximum price. Unfortunately, there are individuals who may park for a

<u>month</u> and claim they "lost" their ticket so that they only have to pay for one day.

With a proper accounting of vehicles in a garage daily and the use of proper technology, any good parking system should be able to recognize if a vehicle was parked for one day or one month, so that an individual cannot steal hours of parking. This is especially critical within an airport parking program where the average length of stay for a vehicle parked may be five days for the casual traveler. Many airports make use of license plate recognition technology (LPR) to take a photo of the license plate of the vehicle entering and exiting which is matched to the time parked on the ticket.

A person should also not be able to walk up to a ticket machine and pull a parking ticket right before departure to minimize his parking cost. This is prevented with the use of metal "loops" embedded in the ground to detect the weight of the vehicle at the entrance and exit of each lane. These are all measures to maintain the integrity of a facilities daily parking revenue.

Doubling Down, Maximizing Use of Space

At a cost in the tens of thousands of dollars per space or even more, parking garages are usually a long-term investment for payback. Most public agencies take out debt (bonds) for a term of 20 to 30 years. Although I am aware of parking garages that are "flipped" within a shorter period by some private parking equity firms, these garages are underperforming based on market conditions and/or have not applied good parking management principles. It is therefore essential to maximize the revenue per parking space. How?

Let us look at an example:

Start with selling a monthly permit for, say, $70 per space per month. That equates to only $3.33 for a 21-day working month or

$3.18 for a 22-day working month. I also call this "reduction to the ridiculous" whenever someone complains about how much it costs to park. I tell them it is $3.33 per day for a full day of parking. Is that too much? No! When you reduce the costs to a daily or even hourly basis, the parking costs are incredibly low.

Your monthly parking fees are your "bread and butter," the foundation for your income. There is usually an absentee factor, meaning that if you have a 100-car garage and sell 100 permits, you would be considered full, right? Well, what happens is a certain percentage of permit holders do not park every day. Some people are on vacation, sick, out of the office on business, and so on. This gives you an opportunity to oversell (overbook), like the airline and hotel industries. To get to a true 100%, you must sell a certain percentage more, based on actual usage numbers of how many cancellations will occur. On occasion, the airlines are wrong and offer vouchers for those willing to book onto another flight. Depending upon your location and demand, this provides you with the opportunity to perhaps sell over the actual number of spaces, maybe starting out at 105 permits and based on actual use, increasing as you are able. So, you can oversell 5% to start, then 10% over time and maximize your use of space and revenue potential. What is the worst that can happen? You fill the garage to capacity, and you redirect vehicles to another garage.

At the same time, daily parking is your "gravy," allowing you to sell spaces at a premium daily rate. The daily rate can be significantly more than the actual daily monthly permit rate. Another factor is that a daily space may turn over two to three times per day versus a permit parker who may park for eight hours per day. As you can see, daily parking is much more lucrative than monthly parking.

These usage patterns fall into an equation as you manage inventory and maximize revenue for each facility, location, and user make up.

THE QUIRKY WORLD OF PARKING | 81

On-Street Demand Based Pricing

The goal for on-street parking is to create turnover for spaces that are in premium demand. Some cities have two-hour maximums or other time limits. Newer strategies include demand-based pricing, also known as dynamic pricing. That is, to not have maximum time limits for parking but rather price the parking based on the demand for that specific block or area and increase the price over time versus chalking and enforcing the time limits.

Demand based pricing can also be used for event parking on nights and weekends near a theater or stadium venue. On-street pricing can be set to coincide with the events time to market rates for that duration.

Demand based pricing provides for a more creative way to generate turnover and revenue in higher demand areas versus the old-fashioned way of across-the-board meter rates and occasional increases. Today, these decisions are based on data that dictates which areas in a city can best accommodate demand based pricing and in what increments. This data is vital in establishing correct parking rates.

Curbside Management

Curbside management is adapting a plan to meet the different needs of users of limited curb space. It is analyzing the best layout for that particular block or area to support all these needs while supporting the ease and flow of traffic.

Those who need curb space include ride share companies like Uber and Lyft (also known as TNC's), commercial and delivery vehicles, bike and scooter parking, pedestrian, and public transportation access for pick up and drop off.

The goal is to analyze actual usage and strategize for solutions to manage the curb and solve specific problems in each block. Put a plan in place to eliminate issues like double parking and create rules and regulations for pick-up, drop-off, and loading zones.

Curbside management may also be an issue when dealing with satellite parking, especially in high demand curb space areas at pick up or drop off locations. This will be discussed in more detail in a following Chapter.

CHAPTER THIRTEEN

SATELLITE PARKING

Satellite parking is usually created when there is insufficient parking on the main grounds of the organization. The most effective and successful satellite (or remote) parking program provides a lower cost option than in the core area. There is a financial incentive to use satellite parking at maybe 50% of core parking costs, and it should provide an efficient transportation program with enough frequency of trips during peak morning and afternoon to not severely prolong an individual's commute. If possible, amenity services should be at the satellite location.

The goal should be to have a satellite lot strategically located within the major routes of those driving to work so that they do not have to go out of their way to access the location. The rationale is to save the driver cost and time. The wait for the ride on a shuttle bus (usually a smaller vehicle under 15 passengers), a regular sized bus (could be a school bus) or a transit fleet bus (40 passenger) should total less time than it would take the driver to find parking in the busy core area.

Depending upon the needs and size of a surface parking lot, locate the satellite in the direction that provides for the most direct path to the core areas. A successful satellite lot should not require an individual heading southerly to drive past the main campus or city, park, then double back to the north on a shuttle to the core area.

The same is true for someone coming from the west and having to drive across town to the east to then take a shuttle back west toward the campus or town.

But it is not unrealistic to drive coming from the north and head east or west and then to the core, same for coming from the south. The point is that a successful satellite operation makes the trip as convenient as possible.

Note, however, that as beneficial as satellite parking is to many drivers, it is rarely profitable. Once you add in all the transportation costs, you will most likely lose money. The loss can either be absorbed into the parking program or the loss can be spread amongst the many entities the satellite parking program serves.

So, if possible, satellite parking should not be viewed as a long-term solution to parking shortages based on the costs needed to run an effective program. Satellite parking can be viewed as pent up demand for parking in closer proximity to the place of employment and justification for creating new surface or structured parking on campus.

The exception in running a profitable satellite program can be found in the many off-airport properties with remote parking facilities. Satellite airport parking has the advantage of charging what market conditions can bear and by handling substantial vehicle volumes in those markets that warrant the demand. Transportation costs are built into the parking fees charged to those customers. Many airport satellite operations also provide amenity services to increase revenues while appeasing their clientele needs.

How an Abandoned Property Became a Satellite Parking Lot and Service Center

When I oversaw parking at a major medical campus, there simply was never enough parking. There was always a need for parking elsewhere to accommodate over 2000 staff and students daily. With these significant numbers, finding the right locations to stage satellite parking was a challenge. The "all good parking lots turn into buildings one day" became a constant theme as properties we had been using were sold off to be developed into a better use than parking. It was typical that within several years of leasing a site, the owners would provide notice that the property was going to be developed into a hotel, residence, or office building. So as we battled with developers and sent real estate agents on covert operations to find available acreage to lease (since it was never prudent to tell a land owner that we were looking to buy property because that knowledge might cause an increase in the price), we decided we needed 1) to control our own destiny and find property that we could purchase and develop for our own long term use, and 2) if possible, improve our core business of providing parking and shuttle services by adding value added services to the program.

Through retreats, brainstorming, and site visits to available properties, we agreed that a satellite parking lot that could provide a car wash and vehicle service center would help busy campus employees multi-task during the work-day and provide one less thing to worry about over the weekend or days off.

After a long and exhaustive search, we focused on eight acres of abandoned land that was once a Ford dealership. The size and proximity (only one mile away from campus) made it an ideal location. Once all environmental concerns were addressed, such as removing old oil and fluid tanks common to a vehicle service center, we purchased the property and moved forward with redevelopment.

Our decision was to demolish the showroom and an auxiliary used-car trailer and reduce the very large service center by about 80%. We would develop half of the structure for departmental use and leave the other half of the building a vacant shell for future use in our vision of a vehicle service complex.

Less than one year later, development of the property was completed. It now accommodates 875 parking spaces, with offices, training facilities, and a comfortable indoor waiting area with vending machines and magazines for drivers all within half the remaining building.

The other half of the building was developed into the car wash and vehicle service center. The service center provides a wide range of automotive services. The center also services all the shuttles and fleet vehicles and is open for public use.

The operation of the car wash and detailing service created a unique opportunity for a community partnership. This was the perfect final piece in creating a best-in-class satellite parking program.

CHAPTER FOURTEEN

LET'S GET THIS PARTY STARTED – OR NOT

Should Garage (Rooftops) Be Leased for Special Events?

"And the winner in the category of Parking Innovation in a Parking Program Goes to the Lancaster Parking Authority for its Garage Roof top Events"

That night I accepted an award for innovation in a parking operation. The next morning, I was brought back down from the euphoria of the win with a presentation by a garage structural engineer titled "Garages are for Parking – Not Parties." I kid you not!

To provide the back story, I had been presented with a beautiful trophy that I cherish and proudly display in my office. With a small mention in our authority newsletter, we had generated a lot of interest and had been very successful in leasing out the roofs of our various garages for different events including a birthday party, political fundraiser, viewing party for downtown fireworks, a tailgate party with antique cars and a "Fire Island" themed fundraiser with dancers, fire breathers, cabanas, DJs, and many bright lights.

I had decided that if we could utilize our parking assets during off-hours "in support of community events" it would be a win-win situation. The events would generate lease revenue as well as parking revenue during off hours. There was also the personal satisfaction seeing people in celebration on a decorated rooftop of a garage and seeing their amazement that a parking garage was transformed into a meeting place and not just a concrete building to park their car in. The adulation from attendees who were not used to such an event also bolstered our image and brand. Many kudos and thanks followed from organizers and attendees. But, no sooner than I was basking in the glow of our award, was I confronted with a presentation about parking garages not being for parties at the conference I was attending. Was this a cruel joke!? I am known as a practical joker, but this went too far, right? But it was the real deal.

My sails started to deflate as an architect from an area consulting engineer firm went through, slide-by-slide, various garage designs and why they should not be designed or used for anything but parking. In one slide, he presented the "total weight of people" as compared to the" total weight of vehicles" in a garage, the total weight of people being much greater than that of vehicles. Agreeing with his mathematical calculations, I had to ask, "Isn't snow much heavier than both?" He agreed that snow was much heavier than both, which went a long way in alleviating the fears of my board members in attendance who were thinking "Are these rooftops events a good idea?" and questioning whether we should continue them. I assured the members that if we do not have hundreds of people jumping up and down in unison to a dance song, the garage would remain sound. Our facilities are old, yet they have survived a small earthquake and yearly fireworks (launched from a platform) being set off from the top of one of our garages for years. Knowing how many millions of dollars I have spent on rehabbing garages over the years, however, I had to ask if there was any historical data on garages being (severely) damaged or collapsing as a result of special events. The presenter stated, "No", but did show several scenes from championship parades where hundreds of spectators crowded along the decks of a garage for a view. (I would have liked the pictures to be from Philadelphia, but they were from Pittsburgh)! Could this number of people create structural damage? There is a strong case that it can. Could someone fall or be pushed over the side? This is a more likely possibility and a dangerous liability situation.

So, should you use your garages for special events and provide a public service to your community? I say the pros outweigh the cons but make sure you take the precautions listed below:

Our insurance company was involved to make sure anyone having an event in our facility had proper insurance coverage and provided a certificate of insurance. Our lawyers were also involved in drafting a good template agreement that anyone leasing the facility needed to sign and abide by. You need to confirm requirements if the event involves liquor. Typically, commercial general liability policies provide "host liquor liability" coverage. That allows you to have an office party with alcohol and serve (free) drinks and still be covered. However, as soon as there is any type of charge associated with liquor, host liquor liability no longer applies. The courts have determined over the years that "selling" alcoholic beverages goes well beyond what the local state store or restaurant does. In fact, "selling" can be a situation where there are drink tickets as part of the admission cost or even requesting donations to offset the price of the alcoholic beverages being supplied. To protect your operation, if the event host(s) intends to provide guests with alcoholic beverages and there is any type of cost or charge associated with that, the host should purchase liquor liability. It may be cost prohibitive, so hopefully anyone leasing the garages will "see the light" and just give it away as part of the event. *Most importantly, make sure no garage personnel are involved with serving, carrying, or otherwise distributing liquor for the event.*

The fire marshal is also contacted to make sure the number of people attending the event does not create a problem and is not a major issue for evacuation. In the event of a fire, you would think anyone can walk down the ramps but you need to have adequate stairway and elevator use if there is a fire.

Operations staff is involved in making sure the logistics of the event are right. I'm stating the obvious, but make sure you emphasize with the event holder that having a party or function on the roof of a parking garage is not the same as having a function in a catering facility. Temporary bathroom facilities need to be provided if none are accessible.

Security needs to be provided to make sure that people are not hanging too close to the edge and not leaving drinks on the ledge. No glass products are allowed, except in poured bottles handled by catering staff. Everything must be paper and plastic since broken glass would be a major problem.

Get a cleaning deposit in addition to the lease to make sure the garage is left "broom clean."

Inform clients that they should plan an alternative location based on inclement weather conditions, which includes too hot/too cold temperatures, rain, wind, etc. Be prepared to relocate the event to a deck below the roof to stay out of the elements. There are better times than others to hold a rooftop event that minimize the impact of weather conditions.

Taking these precautions will help ensure you have successful garage functions that the community will be talking about long after the event is over, while also giving them a different outlook and perspective on parking garages in the future.

CHAPTER FIFTEEN

LIGHTING THE WAY TO SAVINGS

Energy Savings the Easy Way

Budgets for parking organizations across the nation have been strained from declining or flat patronage, steadily rising operating expenses, and increasing maintenance costs. Raising rates can alienate long-time customers, especially in a struggling economy. But that does not mean there are no options to improve the bottom line. One place to look for savings is the lighting systems.

In facilities with older, yellow light (high-pressure sodium (HPS), "T-12") fluorescent lamps or even newer lights (metal halides (MH)), a more efficient system can cut electric and maintenance costs considerably. Tie in a new electricity supply contract (in deregulated states), utility rebates and low-interest financing options, and the picture gets even, pardon the expression, brighter. Done right, the result is not just curtailed operating expenses and a healthier bottom line, but better lighting quality for improved safety and customer comfort and environmental benefits as well.

For many organizations, a smart investment in its lighting system will also reduce energy spending. A novel approach we used was to ask vendors to provide plans for a new lighting system with a turnkey process, along with an electricity supply contract and innovative financing options. Because the power market had fallen since the current agreement was signed a few years before, our authority sought to accomplish two goals with a single contract; 1) to provide a lighting upgrade and, 2) obtain a new multi-year electricity deal. The plan was to keep total expenditure constant and end up with a newer, better lighting system with no cash out-lay, essentially getting a free lighting system.

My authority's garages contained over 1800 fixtures made up of several different systems. Annual energy and maintenance costs were around $200,000. Some facilities were over-lit, others were under-lit, both diminishing the customer experience.

The winning bidder proposed replacing all lights with a fixture designed specifically for parking garages housing the latest, highly efficient, long life T-8 fluorescent lamps. In addition to speeding up installation and cutting project costs, this approach lowered long-term maintenance costs. The fixtures enhanced the garages by providing better illumination which contributes to customer safety and enhances their experience in our garages.

Because of product warranties, initial maintenance costs ended up being zero. The total system wattage was reduced by over 40% and energy costs by nearly half. The energy provider worked closely with the local utility company to maximize the value of a rebate.

Environmental estimates include over 600 tons of CO_2 avoided annually, along with several tons of SO and NO the same as taking over 100 cars off the road or planting over 15,000 trees.

A turnkey project smoothly executed that cuts operating costs, improves safety, provides a better customer experience, and bene-fits the environment, what's not to love.

CHAPTER SIXTEEN

DO NOT STEAL!

Follow the Money Trail

Following the money trail is one of the most important auditing processes in controlling cash and conducting a forensic analysis if an employee is stealing. Following the money trail should start with the payment, whether by cash, credit, on-line, app or other, and follow that payment (ceremonially a dollar) through the collection, deposit, and reconciliation process, including confirmation into the bank account.

There are many check points along the way between the customer payment and bank deposit. Some steps in the process should <u>not</u> be handled by one person. The cash collection should require a separation of duties fulfilled between accounting and operations to secure the integrity and accuracy of all revenue collected. Do not have one person conduct multi space kiosk collections nor count money in a cash room alone. It is best to partner between two parties.

Banking

I have my own personal bank accounts in the same bank as my authority does, because the bank's main office is located close to our parking office, plus I have established relationships with many of the bank managers. I needed to transfer some funds between my two personal accounts. I called the bank to make sure I had enough money to make the transfer. The bank teller said, "Mr. Cohen, you have several million dollars in your account. You'll be fine transferring $4000."

Of course, the millions were in the authority's bank account! Was she going to allow me to transfer parking funds into a personal account? I hope not; but I followed up to make sure that was not possible, even though I am a signer of the parking authority account!

Our good financial planning already requires a co-signor on checks over $10,000. Make sure you do the same.

Financial Hardship

If you deal with handling cash, you have probably had to deal with theft by an employee at some point in your career. I have made it a specific point to always discuss stealing when we hire new employees.

As part of my orientation with new employees, they are sometimes surprised when I bring up the issue and tell them, "Do Not Steal." It is that little dark secret that needs to be exposed. Many of our employees handle cash.

Unfortunately, there have been too many times that there has been theft by one of my better employees. There are various reasons, but addiction and financial hardship seem to be the most prevalent.

I have therefore taken a proactive approach to theft. I say to new employees, that if you are having a financial issue, come to me first, and we will try and help, whether through a loan or advanced salary. But do not come to me after the incident has occurred. At that point, you have lost your job and will be prosecuted if it is deemed appropriate.

I have dealt with many different types of theft. The following are some actual examples.

The Clock is Ticking

Before I arrived at a new job, there was no boss overseeing an employee's daily activities. One employee had a habit of taking a very long lunch break to go to the mall. That person was caught and eventually fired. At that time, that category of salaried employees did not use a time clock, but they did use the time clock going forward.

Not working and going to the mall is stealing. Getting paid and not working is stealing of time. Make sure hourly workers do not have the capability to clock in and out of work for a co-worker. New time management systems, which are more current and sophisticated time clocks, help to solve these types of issues.

Check, Please!

When customers would ask, "Whom do I make the check out to?" An ingenious former employee would tell the customers, "Oh, I'll make the check out for you." Instead of making the check out to our organization or even using our name stamp, she made the check out to herself. Of course, she was easily caught after several months when the customer noticed the parking bill check was made out to an unknown person. Customer service gone wrong!

Can You Spare a Square?

Another employee with an entrepreneurial spirit used our operation to run several businesses out of our office. If that was not bad enough, his businesses provided services back to our organization. He hid his involvement and ownership in the businesses by putting one under the name of a family member and the other under the name of a friend.

When I needed a contractor, this manager sure knew who to hire! His friend was a contractor, and his partner, and they both profited from each project. When I needed a cleaning company, he hired a family member!

But to Mr. Greedy, that was not enough. He ordered cleaning and paper supplies on my dime and then diverted the supplies to one of his companies. At first, I would ask, "What happened to all the toilet paper?" I could not believe we used a case of toilet paper every month for the number of employees we had. Yet, the monthly inventory levels decreased dramatically. With some good sleuth work by our head of finance, we discovered the culprit.

The $120,000 LEGO Room

The worst incident of my career was in my first year on a new job. I caught a manager stealing quarters and bills from on-street multi-space kiosks. He was at the right place at the right time to set up his elaborate scheme to steal. He was at the beginning of implementing the new technology on the street and would be the manager overseeing the repairs of the units and collections. Unfortunately, without proper auditing and key controls in place, he could do the money collections on his own. He siphoned off tens of thousands of dollars over the course of a year and a half.

How did he get caught?

I was a passenger in one of our trucks as we left to do a site visit. My habit has always been to check the glove compartment and arm rest storage area just to make sure nothing illegal is stored in these areas; you never know. Well, I opened the arm rest box and hundreds of dollar bills came flowing out into the truck just like entering an air blown money machine! Yes, we had a problem on our hands.

So how did this crafty manager transport tens of thousands of dollars and coins from the collection routes to his bank account?

He commandeered a storage room in one of our garages. He called it his LEGO room. He stated he loved to play with LEGO's as a relief from working. He would go there during lunch, after work, on the weekends, and dump the coins into a LEGO table, then cover the coins in LEGOS and on occasion transport them to the Coin Star exchange machine at the supermarket. Coins are heavy, so he could only do so many pounds at a time.

Stealing the bills was easier as he hid and transported them from our vehicle to his vehicle. Luckily, the district attorney's office that was handling the case was able to obtain the video showing him dumping the coins for redemption. After a year of pleading innocent, he finally confessed in a plea bargain deal. Unfortunately, he did not get jail time, but he was convicted of a lesser charge that carried restitution and years of probation.

To date, he did pay restitution, but it was nowhere near enough to make up for the theft.

Chicago, Chicago, the Talk of the Town

The largest contract, at the time, awarded for the purchase of multi-space kiosks in the United States was with the City of Chicago for $22 million. It was part of a $1.15 billion dollar deal to privatize all the on-street and off-street parking in the City of Chicago for the next 75 years. In one of the most publicized parking scandals, the $22 million contract for the kiosks was given to a selected vendor who in turn gave a $90,000 kickback to an individual on the selection committee, who was also part of the new parking management team.

Rumblings started occurring when additional kickback money was requested. The FBI caught on to the email exchanges and found out about the illegalities. The sad part is the vendor would have won the award anyway! And off to federal prison went both parties involved. Though he was a well-known warm personality in our profession, this individual would never be allowed back into the industry once he was released from prison. In a crazy twist, he died prematurely in his early fifties from an allergic reaction to a bee sting.

Chicago spent the billion dollars to fund past pensions. The entities overseeing the parking program estimated that they would recoup their investment within ten years. When I visited Chicago and spoke with several principals, they stated that all Chicago had to do was hire competent parking professionals to run the city and they could have created a profitable scenario on its own.

Golf Partners

Another peer in the profession blew his career by playing too much golf with a vendor during working hours. A subordinate employee was the whistleblower. She became disgruntled that her boss was off playing golf too much while she was working. The incident was a headline story on local TV and on the front page of the city paper for many days. Golfing was only one problem, and four top officials at the university had to resign or be fired for violating state and ethics rules.

Obviously, all his bosses were part of the problem by allowing this level of abuse to occur. We too often follow in the footsteps of our boss and think "if it is OK by him, it is OK". But sometimes we need to take a higher ethical stance and tell our boss that this level of conduct is not acceptable! Alas, easier said than done.

I do know that if my boss asked me to play golf three times a week during work hours, I would say "thank you, but I have work to get done". Sometimes we need to show a higher level of conduct and ethics than our boss. Sad but true.

Airport Employees Make the Cash Fly Away

Another highly publicized multi-million-dollar theft by employees involved the Philadelphia airport parking program. It started with parking cashiers. Once the next level supervisor was aware of the theft, he was brought into the scam. Then once the manager was made aware, he was also brought in as well. Multi-level marketing at its best. The point is that it is extremely difficult to uncover theft by employees when so many managers who are entrusted to prevent the theft are involved.

Cash Control?

In my first several months on the job at the authority, I stopped in to talk to the former finance manager and found piles and piles of bills covering the entire desk and overflowing onto the surrounding floor after a day of multi-space kiosk collections. It looked like scene out of the movie *Ritchie Rich*. Needless to say, it was not the epitome of cash control, and I knew I had a laundry list of issues to address.

The 80-10-10 Rule

Throughout my career, I have always been cognizant of the 80-10-10 rule. It may be somewhat controversial, but it breaks down like this: 10% of your employees are super honest and would never steal under any scenario, 10% will try to steal under every scenario; and 80%, will generally conform to the policies, procedures and rules of the organization, but may sway to the dark side and take financial advantage based on how your organization is run. Stealing might begin with pens and pencils but become more serious over time.

A prominent owner of a parking company said, "If you do not do your job, you can make a thief out of an honest employee."

CHAPTER SEVENTEEN

PARKING AND COVID-19

When discussing the COVID-19 pandemic, we must first and foremost recognize the significant loss of life. This should never be forgotten. So, discussing parking in this context seems trivial, yet my goal is to outline the business impact and discuss how we were able to support the recovery during such a tragic time in our lives.

Since I am writing this book during the pandemic in 2020, I could not avoid discussing its impact and the positive change that the use of parking areas has achieved.

Like most businesses, when the pandemic hit in March 2020, we were forced to close a large percentage of our business. No longer were we providing significant monthly and daily parking and enforcement; it was sidelined while everyone was in a shelter-in-place scenario for several months.

At the end of the month of April 2020, we had lost nearly 95% of our revenue. Employees in the city were no longer coming to work, whether they were laid off or working from home. Our convention center and all theaters were closed. Schools were closed. No one was dining out anymore. And we had significant financial losses of multi-million dollars in lost revenue.

I truly felt the pain that businesses were going through, and I had hoped that something between solving the pandemic and keeping businesses open was attainable. Our revenue losses had a domino effect: facilities could not be repaired, many of our employees lost their jobs, and construction was brought to a halt.

Most businesses faced significant financial losses during COVID-19, including the parking industry. The questions regarding parking will have a major economic impact on all cities.

The questions I get asked the most are:

Will parking demand return to cities?
Or, will everyone now work from home?

I respond by saying that the worst case from our business perspective is no one returns to work and everyone continues to work from home, which will eliminate the need for parking and office space. There will be a subsequent impact on restaurants, shopping, and the entire economic recovery of cities.

On the other side of the equation, everyone returns to work, more employees might not be inclined to use public transportation, ride share services, and other transportation modes; and the demand for parking would increase dramatically.

My best estimate is the impact lands somewhere in the middle and provides a good balance when there is a full recovery, which may take several years. But strong businesses positioned to survive the ups and downs of the economy will survive, cities that were doing well will bounce back, and employees will return to the office environment.

The parking business will survive but with less dependence on staff and more dependence on technology that lowers operating expenses and provides post COVID-19 touchless opportunities to pay and park.

Rats are Everywhere!

One of the driving forces in bringing enforcement back into operation during the pandemic was streets that were typically cleaned by street sweepers several times per month was not occurring.

Enforcement's role is to follow the street sweepers and ticket those vehicles that have not been moved so that the streets can be cleaned. When statistics from the city got out that the rat and vermin population was exploding onto the streets because debris and food were accumulating, it was time for enforcement to commence again. Thank you, rats!

The Touchless Experience

Paying for parking has also changed, expedited by the pandemic. People do not want to touch things in the public domain unless required. Credit cards have gone from swiping to tapping, and that change in the retail world is cascading out to the payment of parking transactions and for access to parking garages and buildings. Tapping in proximity to a door or gate is taking the place of swiping a card.

Even more recently, some parking hardware and software manufacturers have developed the use of hand identification. A monthly customer can now access their parking by holding their hand in proximity to the entry and exit equipment instead of using an access card.

The Cashless Environment

Especially during COVID-19, we have asked ourselves: *"How can we reduce our cash sales and provide better customer service and more efficiency and revenue integrity in the process?"*

The answer is by:

- Reducing lines at the cashiers in the garages

- Speeding up transaction times in the garages

- Creating less paperwork with less tickets sales

- Reducing staff

- Reducing potential theft by taking the transactions out of a cashier's hands

These are some of the benefits to the organization as well as to the customer.

Parklets

The one thing that was quickly realized was the need to support restaurants who faced limited inside seating capacity based on the mandates from some states.

This is where parking programs have come to the rescue; in using on-street parking and converting these spaces into outside dining parklets for widespread public use. Basically, restaurants have turned parking spaces into outside dining parklets. These parklets allow restaurants to use parking spaces for outside dining, as limitations were put on capacity within their businesses. In some areas, we were able to close the entire street and create a food court type of environment. Restaurants located without the capacity to provide outside seating nearby found the food court plan works well.

Although eliminating parking spaces that could generate thousands of dollars per year, it is the right thing to do in support of the survival of many restaurants.

Curbside Pick Up

On-street parking spaces are also serving as additional loading zones to support restaurants providing curbside pick-up for customers and food service delivery companies. It is important to maintain on-street enforcement to make sure these spaces are turning over and are free for this critical need during COVID-19.

Fix the Crack!

Those parking programs with good financial reserves are taking advantage of this time with emptier garages to conduct repairs. Some airport parking garages that would usually be at capacity are now conducting repairs with minimal impact on travelers and fewer changes of traffic patterns. Fewer customers, but more repairs. Basically, taking advantage of the opportunity that is presented in difficult times.

Most of us are not so lucky with negative revenue impact so severe that capital repairs, capital upgrades and even building new parking structures are being deferred for another year or two to make sure economic recovery occurs.

Parking Garages to the Rescue – Part I

When COVID-19 was spiking across the United States, hospitals were transforming parking garages into triage and patient care units. At least one health system turned an entire facility into a COVID-19 patient care unit. The multi-day transformation from a parking garage to a unit that can handle more than 1400 patients was incredible. The plan was that COVID-19 patients would be moved to the garage unit when they were stable and improving.

It is wonderful to know that parking assets can play a vital role in the recovery and can have a positive impact.

Parking Garages to the Rescue – Part II

Parking lots around the country were being used to stage for COVID-19 testing sites and subsequent administration of the vaccine. It is great to see parking lots serving this vital role in recovery, but I am sure we will all be happy when places like Dodger Stadium will return to parking cars for baseball games versus playing this vital role in the pandemic recovery.

CHAPTER EIGHTEEN

THE CRAZY SIDE OF PARKING

There are many crazy stories that I have accumulated throughout the years that are worthy for inclusion in my book. If I had known I would be writing a book after 40 years in the parking business, I might have kept better notes of the incidents that occurred along the way. I would have many more stories if I could remember more! So, if you want to write a book one day, start taking notes early in your career.

Won't You Be My Neighbor?

We moved into a new neighborhood in Maryland. Routinely, on a nice day, I might be in my driveway washing my car. One day a neighbor several houses away walked by and asked if I worked in the parking business. My vanity license plate said PARKING so that may have given it away, although some people thought the plate stood for Par-King. I could only wish I were a par golfer, not even close!

My neighbor revealed he also oversaw parking, at another local university. What were the odds that two parking professionals lived on the same block, two doors away! Pretty crazy and always a fun story to tell.

Sinkhole

Do you have sufficient emergency, contingency and continuity plans? I hope so. The head of another authority came into work to find her office building had fallen into a large sink hole! Luckily, no one was hurt, and they were eventually able to retrieve valuable records and computers. But if your offices had experienced a similar or worse fate, how hard would it be to re-establish operations?

Our programs are usually covered for instances like weather emergencies, but make sure you have the same type of plans for your IT systems (be cloud based) and other important aspects of your operation. Even hope-they-never-happen scenarios like riots need an emergency plan, such as, if the riots move into your facilities and vandalism and destruction occur.

Detailed emergency, continuity, and contingency plans are like peeling the layers of an onion, the more you uncover, the deeper the areas that need attention and planning. Many, many, hours of work will be needed. Be prepared for your sink hole!

The Watergate

While working in Washington, DC, one of our parking garages was below the former Howard Johnson's restaurant and hotel (HoJo's as it used to be called). Nothing strange there, but the hotel above the Howard Johnson's and our parking garage was located directly across the street from the Watergate apartments, which is famous for the wiretapping of the phones of the democratic party headquarters during the President Nixon years.

The illegal wiretapping eventually led to Nixon's resignation. Most interesting is that the hotel rooms in HoJo's had been converted to dormitory rooms, except for one, one room used for the wiretapping. There is even a plaque on the door. Do not worry, we checked. No wiretapping in the garage, at least that I knew about.

Sacred Burial Grounds

While under construction, a garage project excavation came across a potential sacred burial site where skeletal remains were found. The project was derailed for over six months until the remains were removed, and a proper relocation site was agreed upon by the clergy involved. Is this a case for a haunted garage?

A Baseball Player, A Porsche, and an Illegal Substance

Along with my success at Veterans Stadium, I ended up providing valet services at many other events throughout the Philadelphia region. One of those events was a charity event, hosted by the Phillies baseball team. Most players were involved in this golf outing, and luckily my company was hired to provide our services at the event. I took part myself with my best employees. Everything was going great until the end of the event.

A famous Phillies player had his car retrieved and was screaming that something was missing out of his car. I was terrified about this accusation and asked if I could take an incident report. He emphatically said No. I questioned my staff, who all stated that they had no idea what he was talking about, and the issue never came up again until years later. When I sold the business and had a going away party, one of my most trusted employees confessed to me that he had taken a large bag of marijuana out of the player's glove compartment! I was glad he confessed because it was confirmation that it was time to sell the business – too many kids taking advantage of a good situation.

Over the years, I had to deal with joy riding, theft of items from vehicles, and accidents. Remember the *Fast Times at Ridgemont High* valet scene? Yes, that is an exaggeration of reality, but it is real to a point. I knew it was my time to move on.

Best Employee Excuse

I had an employee who was caught kissing another employee in the stairs. She was going to be suspended and she filed an appeal with the union. When she was brought in for questioning with management and the union representative, her response was, "I kissed him, but I promise I did not f*ck him." I said, okay, probably too much information (TMI). Her suspension was upheld.

Worst Customer Excuse

Those of us in the business have heard this excuse too many times to count. Someone who has received a parking citation says, "I don't have money to pay for a ticket." What they are really saying is, "I don't want to spend my money to pay for a parking ticket when I could use my money to pay for anything else in life other than a parking ticket."

The Winner Is...

Every year the front page of our local paper used to list the largest dollar amount offenders in receiving parking tickets for the previous year. And every year it was the same attorney, who would be parked right outside his office and basically receive a citation every day. To him, it was the cost of a reserved space outside his door and the value of not wasting time parking legally and walking to his office from the garage. When asked for a quote on being the yearly leader in citation revenue, his response was, "I should not be called out for receiving the citations, since I always pay all the tickets. I should be commended for my contributions to the city and parking authority. The paper would be better served in listing those who do not pay their tickets." Touché! I cannot disagree.

Fake Facebook

Be aware of fake Facebook or other social media sites. A clever fellow created a fake Facebook account for our authority. It looked real enough, but the posted information was wrong. Though his posts were pretty much harmless, being in the same satiric vein as *The Onion,* I was still unamused as the site mislead the public who viewed it.

Parking Obituary

We received a complaint from a family member that their car had received numerous parking tickets for a family member who died. People make up various excuses all the time, so we checked the obituary just to validate the death. It seems harsh, but it works.

My Parking Obituary

Not to contradict the seriousness of the topic of death, which I have addressed herein, but on the lighter side I have contemplated what my obituary would read.

In our life planning, we should all spend time writing our will, whether we are 30 years old with limited assets or approaching retirement age. This perpetuated a conversation with my wife, and we joked about what my obituary might say:

Larry J. Cohen, Parking Expert

People would read it and say, "Parking expert? You can be an expert in parking a car?"

I guess I will have to stick with *loving husband and father.*

Bad Fertilizer

I spent nearly a decade in Washington, D.C. I worked six blocks from the White House and next to the World Bank, so security was always paramount. All underground parking garages not only had gate arms for access but roll down security gates. Many buildings also had security personnel watching over the buildings and garage access.

We simulated many different emergency situations over the years; the worst of the worst type of situations and how we would play a role in either parking or transportation to support any emergency or recovery efforts from a catastrophic event. In my many years, we were fortunate to only deal with simulated situations.

Imagine my surprise when I left Washington, and headed to Lancaster, Pennsylvania, that I encountered an emergency I never thought I would experience in a small town.

I approached the border of town and was trying to get to my office when I found the entire city in lockdown. There was a bomb threat in one of my garages! It housed my office and was next to the county building. From my training and simulations over the years, I set up a remote office at my board chairman's office on the edge of town and handled our operation from this remote location, which was hastily put together.

It appeared that three trucks were lined up on different levels of the garage, with fertilizer on the bed of each truck. Maybe a normal occurrence in Lancaster or not. I was never able to confirm with the FBI, nor would they discuss with me, whether it was a legitimate threat or not.

Friendly Fire

Another interesting experience in central Pennsylvania occurred when I was sitting in my office and heard gunshots from the garage roof. I discovered that every year a group of volunteers fired pellet gunshots off the garage to divert the migratory practices of crows that, in the past, would come to nest in areas of the garage. Pigeons fall into this same category. Every year we would get permission from this volunteer group for this activity. As far as I know, no crows or pigeons have been injured or killed.

Pigeon Droppings

Have you ever seen metal spikes coming up from the concrete surrounding a parking garage? They are put in place to keep pigeons from nesting and to prevent their acidic droppings from landing on your car or head as you wait for the elevator or retrieve your car.

I was once told that cheese curls laced with poison had been used to "remove" pigeons before the advent of spikes. I would rather use the spikes.

Fireworks

We set fireworks off the roof of one of our garages in a dense downtown area. Really. Give the fire department and pyrotechnical company credit. It occurs every year without any incident of a fire in the surrounding neighborhood and does not cause any seismic damage to the garage. Fingers crossed and knock on wood, we have been doing this for over ten years without an incident and to the delight of the community.

Hunting Season

I am not a hunter and was raised as a city boy. So, when I came into work one day during my first year outside a major city, I was shocked that almost half my staff was off from work. I had no idea that the first day of hunting season was like a state holiday. Schools were even closed. This city boy learned quickly about hunting season. I even feasted for the first time on a deer steak and jerky. It tasted o-k.

Watermelon Man

It is dangerous enough to be monitoring the roofs of our garages for potential suicides or other nefarious activities, but somehow others look to get enjoyment from throwing things off the roof. One gentleman (or idiot) thought it would be amusing to drop a water-melon off the roof of a seven-story garage, i.e., a David Letterman routine from the 1980's. The watermelon struck a car exiting the garage and caused the vehicle significant damage. Fortunately, the driver was uninjured, although visibly shaken, and no pedestrian was harmed. That watermelon could have killed someone. The Police were happy to handle this incident.

Nuts and Bolts

Another teenager thought it would be fun to throw nuts and bolts from the roof of the garage across the street at diners eating outside. Luckily, he did not have the accuracy needed to hit someone and possibly cause serious injury. We had him arrested.

Porta Potties

As many cities experience, dealing with the homeless population is a constant challenge. It is difficult to find a balance of initiatives that both respect those individuals, and their possible mental health issues, and serves the best interest of the community.

I have worked over the years to support these efforts, but I cannot say very successfully. I volunteered, as a stop gap measure, to put several Porta Potties in one of my garages while the city tried to figure out a permanent solution. As soon as you think you have resolved the issue in the short term, you learn there is no simple answer. Instead of using the Porta Potties, several in our homeless community defied the solution and instead consistently defecate in front of the portable toilets. Sadly, this constant battle continues to this day.

Long Distance Parking

We had a multi-space kiosk that was doing phenomenally revenue-wise. This kiosk was doing twenty times the revenue of any other kiosk in the city. It was so good that we could not believe it was true. Well, it was too good to be true. When we delved further, many transactions in $5 increments were being posted to the machine. It was strange because we did not have a $5 fee!

After discussions with the kiosk vendor, we discovered that the fees from another kiosk in another state were coming to our machine. The other machine was located at a transit stop with a flat $5 payment. The kiosk manufacturer had made a software error which diverted the funds to us instead of to the town with the malfunctioning kiosk. Because that town rarely audited the machines, this money transfer went on for nearly six months!

When we alerted the out-of-staters and told them we wanted to return the money, they insisted on a legal agreement being completed first. For us to return the money we had volunteered to send them! We eventually returned the money. Afterwards, the kiosk manufacturer had to make up the difference in our lost revenue to us.

Construction Gone Bad

Because many millions of dollars are spent designing and building parking facilities, when a garage is completed and open for business you would hope that it would function appropriately. Not always.

- One new garage had the entrance too low because of a misplaced beam. The solution? Chip away the new slab of concrete at the entrance lane to bring the clearance back.

- In another, when I was driving towards the exit, the car bottomed out, scraping the whole underside. The slope in the garage was too severe for any speeds above VERY SLOW.

- In another, the entrance lane was too narrow to fit cars entering and exiting at the same time. The solution? Put up bright orange plastic bollards, (i.e., poles), to delineate the entrance and exit lanes. Spend millions of dollars on a project and then need to fix it with $100 in fancy traffic cones!

- I once walked up the stairs in a sparkling new facility and hit my head on an overhead light. I am 5' 8", not 6' 6". Perhaps the lights were hung too low?

The moral of these not-funny-at-the-time stories is that someone with an operations background should be involved in the designing of a new garage along with the architects and engineers. The design might look good (architects) and be put together well (by engineers), but, as my saying goes, the operations guys will "take the keys to the building and drive it for the next 30 years." Make sure the garage is functional!

I Need a (New) Doctor

What do an accountant and a doctor have in common? No real punch line here.

LIFO is an accounting term usually used to describe inventory, meaning Last In, First Out, as opposed to FIFO, meaning First In, First Out. One sells the oldest inventory first or the newest inventory first.

This accounting principle played a different but similar role in a strategy to relocate parkers off a surface lot to make way for new development. The surface lot was in a prime location that was targeted for redevelopment into a parking garage and office space for a medical center tower. To make this project happen, the 400 employees parking on the lot would need to be relocated. Most of the staff parking on this prime lot location were doctors, nurses, and their support staff next to their outpatient center building. Unfortunately, there was not enough space on the rest of the campus to accommodate and relocate everyone to other parking close to their work location since the most important goal was to maintain enough parking for patients and visitors.

How does a campus handle this situation? Answer: with many negotiations between the various entities of the campus, including the hospital, Schools of Medicine, public health, and nursing.

A plan was devised for employees to move to remote satellite parking (which was discussed) and take a bus to work. Not ideal for those used to parking right next to the building they worked in!

It was mutually agreed that employees most recently hired, i.e., with the least seniority, would be the first to be relocated; in other words, LIFO. However, doctors and other clinical care providers were exempt from LIFO. The criteria of LIFO morphed into LIFO with exceptions. Support staff would relocate; anyone with 24-hour clinical care responsibilities would not.

When word got around that this was the agreed upon and fairest method for relocation, I thought the hardest part was done. No way!

Employees came out of the woodwork with a myriad of reasons why they could not possibly relocate. Some were substantiated but most were trivial excuses. My staff were bombarded with so many irate complaints that they threatened to quit because of the constant abuse. We then required that those demanding a relocation waiver present doctor verification that riding a bus to work would be harmful to their health. Of course, working at a hospital, they all had access to a doctor. We had to solicit the support of the occupational health department to determine legitimate claims. It got to the point of determining what type of pregnancy a women might have, whether high risk or not.

Perhaps the worst part for me was that my doctor whom I had seen for many years started faxing me (before texting!) all the time, maybe 20 faxes to get my attention, that his secretary had to stay on-site and not relocate. When I told him she could not stay, and we moved her, I had to change doctors because my comfort level with him had diminished drastically; he would not stop complaining about the decision to relocate his secretary! Our deteriorated relationship was another casualty of the politics of parking.

No Reservation Needed

Just as I had to seek a new doctor, there are many restaurants I do not feel comfortable eating at anymore. Over the years, I have had conflicts with some restauranteurs about their parking situation or issuing parking citations to customers. Some felt they had to vent their issues in a public forum, not even providing me a chance to rectify the issue. When these conflicts occur, I swear off eating at their establishments. Call it a grudge or not wanting my food tampered with. Currently, there are at least four very successful restaurants I will no longer patronize. I believe at some point there will be nowhere left for me to eat in the city. A new weight loss program!

Motorcycles

After a long hibernation over the winter, spring arrives and so do motorcycles. If you want to drive a parking operator crazy, drive a motorcycle into a parking facility. Entrances and exits of parking garages and lots with gate arms are triggered by the weight of the vehicle on a metal loop in the ground. Many motorcycles do not weight enough to trigger the loop that activates the monthly permit or ticket machine. So what does a good motorcycle rider do? If possible, they drive around the gate arm and park for free, because they can also drive around the gate arm at the exit.

The situation got so bad, that one city fought to have motorcycles banned from using its parking facilities and only allow them to park on the streets. I was president of the local parking association at the time (the Middle Atlantic Parking Association), and the local newspaper sought a quote from me. After alerting the Executive Director of the Parking Authority that I had been dragged into this issue, my official response was, "Motorcycles should have to pay like everyone else. Whatever actions need to be taken should be allowed."

Since that time, the authority has continued to allow motorcycle parking by enhancing the weight sensitivity to capture motorcycles entering and exiting and extended the garage gate arms so motorcycles could not go around them.

Job Interview

I was a candidate for a high-profile parking job. Many of my friends in the industry told me *not* to be a candidate for the position. They thought true reform and changes could not be made because of the city's political environment and that I was better suited for an operation where I could make real substantive changes.

It ended up being the most unusual selection process of my career. The time from my initial conversation with the headhunter to a final decision was ten months. After my in-person interview with their board, and several months had passed, I was doing a presentation with my parking peeps at a conference. Those in attendance included staff from that organization. In the middle of the presentation, my phone started to "blow up." (Yes, you should turn off your phone when you are doing a presentation).

After the presentation, I immediately checked my messages. The first call was from the city's major newspaper. The reporter stated that I was going to be named the new head of the organization. The next three calls were from my local state representative's offices telling me that same paper was calling for a quote on my hiring. There were also numerous views on my LinkedIn profile from employees of that organization.

There was only one problem. I had heard nothing about this supposedly imminent opportunity. Even the headhunter overseeing the search was shocked and had no idea what was going on.

They swore that nothing was leaked to the press and that I had not been offered the job. Although, I believe it may have been leaked by a board member to gauge acceptance of the hire within the community.

To this day, I really do not know what happened, just conspiracy theories, since I was not offered the job. Whether the hiring was based on political machinations or not, it was not meant to be.

By the way, the city ended up hiring a politico who did not meet all the job requirements; But I will say from afar that he has done a good job in a very tough political environment. Sometimes the best jobs are the ones you do not get.

Games People Play

People are always trying to find ways to not pay for parking. I found it amusing that with the advent of mobile app payments, individuals try to find ways to "game" the system. An individual will park on the street and not pay for parking. As soon as the PEO approaches the area, they quickly pay for 10 minutes of parking on the app. This is usually enough time until the PEO walks past their vehicle. I assume this is done 3 to 4 times per day based on our typical enforcement block.

I don't know about you, but I have better things to do than be on the lookout for a PEO throughout the day to save less than $10 in parking costs.

C H A P T E R   N I N E T E E N

SUMMER VACATION

How I Spent a Summer Visiting Parking Garages in Italy

Posted on the bulletin board in my office is a clipping that says, "When I retire, I want to see the country, one ballpark at a time..." Based on a trip to Italy to visit parking facilities, I may need to re-title it, "When I retire, I want to see the world, one parking facility at a time..."

The trip occurred for an evaluation of a company based in Cesena, Italy. They have had very good success with building cylindrical, fully automated, underground parking facilities in Italy. Seeking potential markets in the United States, the company approached a non-profit organization called the Civil Engineering Research Foundation (CERF) based in Washington, D.C. They asked CERF to provide 1) an in-depth, unbiased evaluative report on the company's technology that could be provided to architects, engineers, builders, and others throughout the United States and 2) a testament of the legitimacy of the technology as part of new parking projects.

CERF gathers expert panels in various professions to evaluate new technologies, including bridge foundations, signs, highway signs and road paving materials. CERF contacted my peer organization and other organizations for potential panel members. A broad range of members was chosen that comprised a cross section of parking operators, finance experts, architects, builders, and engineers.

Once the panel was selected, we spent two days at CERF headquarters evaluating every aspect of the Italian company's engineering, operations, construction, and financing. These two days resulted in a draft report of our findings. Even with the report, however, the committee still had many issues that needed to be answered. The consensus was that we still needed to "kick the tires" before we bought into the concept of fast and efficient underground automated parking garages.

Automated garages date back to the early 1900's. This is not an entirely new technology, but one that has evolved from elevator lifts, prominently in the Northeast. Now there are automated garages scattered across the country. Are we on the verge of a resurgence of automated garages in the 21st century?

There is still a great deal of reluctance when it comes to automated garages; cost and reliability are major concerns. Being a natural skeptic, I welcomed the opportunity of a site visit to alleviate my operational concerns.

Once the report was issued, almost a year had passed since the panel reconvened. To our surprise, the company agreed with our suggestion that a site visit was warranted. The staff members would provide tours, starting at the offices in Cesena.

Try telling your family, co-workers, boss, and friends that you are going to Europe to visit parking garages. Responses range from "Huh?" to "Are you OK?" to "Yeah, right." If nothing else, it was a great icebreaker at a party!

Upon arriving in Italy, I met up with the other panel members who were able to make the trip. Jet lag and all, we geared up for the real test – legitimizing the claims of automated parking facilities.

The company is a multi-million dollar enterprise that provides many services in manufacturing and construction throughout the world. After initial greetings and tours, we went to work where we had left off in the CERF offices; examining the same persistent issues. The only way to alleviate our concerns would be the visits.

We spent an exhaustive two days visiting many different operations in Cesena. Some were "permit only" parking; others were "mixed-use" permit and daily pay. It was an amusing observation to see parking professionals with a combined 100+ years of experience, watching in amazement as one car after another entered the facility and disappeared beneath the surface. Most of the patrons (monthlies) would not even look back as they entered the building and their vehicle disappeared below the street surface.

The other notable observation was the extreme contrast between old and new. Many of the buildings in Cesena are over 200 years old; yet, in the town center is a 21st century parking facility that in a very unusual way, fits in to create open space.

We were very impressed with the company and the high level of service provided by the automated garages. Retrieval times were consistently between one to two minutes per vehicle. With the help of a translator, we were able to interview many customers. Most were very pleased with all aspects of the service. The most negative comments were from first-time users who needed help navigating the process; Help, however, was only an intercom call away to a central communication center. Users were also pleased with the inherent security and elimination of weather elements by having their vehicles stored underground.

Automated parking is not a system for every parking solution; but at the right locations with the right user group, it can be an effective solution to parking problems. Think about the positive outcomes, valet parking without valets and condominium owners with a touchless reserved parking experience.

The irony is that automated elevator parking has been used in densely populated cities like New York for many years. It is kind of like the phrase, "What's old is new again?" It was a privilege to observe the "new wave" of parking technology, one for the 21st century.

CHAPTER TWENTY

ON THE FRONT LINES OF PARKING

Interviews

Some of the wisest advice I have ever received about inter-viewing prospective employees, is that the day of the interview will be the best you will ever see them, and to note carefully how they react and answer your questions.

The first question I always ask is, "What do you know about us?" It is really an easy softball question for those who took ten minutes or so to review our website. It shows their initiative and how interested they really are in a position within your organization.

Employees in Transition

I have taken great pride in our effort over the years to hire eligible employees who were once homeless or living in a shelter. We provided them an entry level job as a cashier or parking atten-dant to help them move their life in a positive direction. There is no greater personal satisfaction in playing a part in someone's personal transition and growth. All these types of hires do not have a positive outcome, but the ones that work out are incredibly fulfilling.

Asking the Right Questions

Any of us who have hired front line staff over the years find one of the most challenging aspects of the job is getting good candidates. I have hired hundreds of employees through the years and it never gets easier. Most employees fall into four categories: 1) those just starting to work after high school, 2) retired individuals seeking employment to supplement income, 3) those seeking a second job to support a family, and 4) lost souls needing a job until they can figure out their next step in life.

There is no profile of a perfect parking attendant or other staff. The key is asking the right questions to determine if the candidate is the right fit for that particular job.

Open ended questions allow you to get answers to better understand the candidate. Questions such as:

- Tell me about a time you had to overcome a major obstacle.

- Tell me about your approach in dealing with difficult customers.

And for a higher-level position, ask a more detailed and complex open-ended question such as:

- Tell me about some of the most difficult problems you worked on and how you solved them?

From this question alone, you should be able to ascertain whether the candidate was responsible, or someone else was more responsible.

Customer Service in 10 Seconds

When I meet with potential or new employees, I take out a blank piece of paper and one-by-one I draw eyes, a smile, and a thank you or an abbreviated "TY!" I tell them that if the only things you provide to a customer are eye contact, a smile, and a thank you, then they have provided good customer service. (Pardon my artistic skills.)

Eyes and Ears

"See something, say something". This saying has been around for many years. I first saw it on a Washington subway nearly 20 years ago. The simple message still holds true today. We should remind our staff to be aware of their surroundings. If they see something that looks out of place (an individual, package, vehicle, or something else) they must report it to their supervisor.

Ingrained in us hundreds of years ago is a perfect gauge of suspicion; when the hairs on the back of your neck stand up, warning us something might be very wrong.

Help! I'm Being Carjacked!

I used to oversee a small surface lot, with a cashier, as one of my properties at Johns Hopkins Medical campus which is set in an urban environment. One of our staff was almost the victim of a carjacking right off campus. She was stopped at a stop light when someone approached the car and tried to open her door. The intruder could not get into her car because she had her doors locked. When the police took her statement, she stated that she had her doors locked because the parking cashier every night when she left work would tell her, "Don't forget to fasten your seat belt and lock your doors."

A simple yet powerful story about how front-line staff _can_ make a difference every day. This is one of the stories I have shared throughout the years with newly hired front-line employees.

A Night at the Theater

We have a performing arts theater in town that use one of our garages. Every show has a Playbill. A Playbill is usually a yellow and black program that lists the actors and others involved in the production. One of our cashiers took it upon herself that when patrons are leaving the garage after a show has ended, to ask them if they enjoyed the performance. Some customers ask, "How did you know I attended the show?"

She replied, "I see the Playbill on your seat!" Just another example of a nice gesture by an employee going above and beyond in a transaction.

9/11

All Americans over the age of 30 knows where they were on 9/11. I lost a high school classmate and the brother of another acquaintance on that day.

I was at work. When word got out about the attacks, we all watched the unfolding events on a wheeled in TV. As I worked at a major hospital close to Washington, we were put on alert to have transportation available to transport doctors and nurses in support of the rescue efforts. Tragically, we did not send the doctors and nurses, because there were many deaths, but not many survivors. I wish we could have played a part in the recovery so that we felt we had helped. Unfortunately, there was nothing we could do.

Survey Says...

Typically, once a year, we have a customer appreciation day. I deploy my staff at all our garage entrances and greet every customer entering. We provide them with a small gift and a wrapped breakfast bar and ask them to fill out our on line survey for a chance to win a gift card to an area restaurant. When we survey our customers, we ask about the following areas:

✓ Friendliness of Staff

✓ Cleanliness of Facilities

✓ Ease of Access and Exiting

✓ Ease of Finding a Space

✓ Clear & Concise Signs for Pedestrians & Vehicles

✓ Ease of Payment

✓ Safe and Secure

And then a comment section.

Your customers will have no problem telling you what is wrong. But sometimes there are valid suggestions amongst the typical complaints. Consider them and put a plan in place to address those issues.

CHAPTER TWENTY-ONE

PARKING AND THE MEDIA

Parking Wars

Parking Wars was a very highly rated cable show on the Art and Entertainment (A&E) Network for many years, showing the day-to-day interactions within a parking authority. The show mostly revolved around the Philadelphia Parking Authority (PPA), but later moved on to other cities. A peer at the time at PPA stated they were never excited about having a television show following their daily activities, but a yearly donation from A&E to the mayor's office meant the show continued for many seasons.

The show was everyone's perception of working at a parking authority; the good and not so good employees, crazy customers, ticketing, towing, and impounding vehicles. Many people ask if I watched the show. Maybe for 5 minutes every so often. It was too much like going to work. Why would I want to watch a show that reminds me of going to work?!

The Press

My first experience with the press was when I was eight years old and won the highest-flying kite contest held every summer in my hometown. It was very cool to see a picture of myself in the local paper!

My experiences with the press continued as I read the stories about my favorite sports teams and followed and admired many sports writers through my youth. I even spent time as a sports reporter doing blurbs for local high school sporting events and was the public address announcer at football games. So, I always had a favorable impression of the press.

My good luck with the press continued after I had worked my way through high school and college and started my own parking company at age 23. Along the way, I thought it would be a good idea to try and franchise my parking company versus a more traditional path of growth through expanding valet operations and managing parking properties. In hindsight, I should have expanded our management services versus trying to franchise a business that is not an ideal model, since only one franchise would encompass an entire city or territory.

Regardless, I was able to get national exposure in *Income Plus* and *New Business Opportunities* magazines. I was an Ernst and Young's Young Entrepreneur finalist and a Pennsylvania Small Business award winner. All great press. "Young entrepreneur started in his parent's basement with $3000" made a good story.

As I moved into the university and hospital sector, most press interaction was more like public relations. It included good stories about how parking, transportation, and transportation options benefitted both students and employees.

Student newspapers, however, generally did not give much space to parking related stories. They were more concerned about the happenings in student government.

Later, at the start of my career in a municipal authority, a local reporter wrote an amazing life story article about me before I arrived in town. The only disturbing thing was that he printed my salary. Printing salaries of public officials is a great way to increase readership; the paper used to publish a yearly list of salaries of public officials.

It is not great for someone like me who likes to keep his private life private, but one of the biggest changes in the municipal world is the Right to Know law that states that the public has a right to request some documents of an authority, and those of city, county, state, or federal government. Just fill in a Right to Know request form, and the government entity is obligated to deliver the information within a certain number of business days.

Sensationalism

The facts of a news story depends mostly on the reporter, but its tone and <u>which</u> facts are presented are mostly on the editor. Most newspapers, print or on line, and their readers, do not like parking authorities and the work we conduct. Thus, there is sometimes an inherent adversarial relationship. You may spend an hour talking to a reporter, and then the editor picks out the several words that will create his desired headline to increase readership.

I believe the worst case of our local newspaper sensationalizing a story was when they provided a dotted line diagram of how a suicide plunged. It was just before my tenure, but I saw the clipping and it was terrible.

So, it is important to keep pushing the positive stories to the press to offset the negative ones.

TV

Dealing with television reporters is quite different than dealing with newspaper reporters. A newspaper article may be a lengthy interview with many details, even graphs and sidebars with statistics, but a TV interview is all about the sound bite. Local news is fast and giving you 10 to 20 seconds of airtime in a twenty-two-minute newscast is the norm. Therefore, you must learn to adapt and position yourself differently when commenting for a newspaper story versus for a television story.

I have relationships with some local TV reporters. When they show up for a quote, they say I know the drill. I give them the 10 to 20 seconds they require, and the interview is done.

CHAPTER TWENTY-TWO

THE HIGHS...

Giving Back

Organizations around the country have done a fantastic job, especially during the holidays, to provide opportunities to redeem parking tickets for items needed to support those in need. I have sponsored two programs that "give back" to the community.

Toys for Tickets

Toys for Tickets is a program we ran for many years at George Washington University. It allowed anyone with an outstanding parking citation to pay off the current value of the ticket— including any late payment fees that had accrued—with a new, unwrapped toy or toys of equal or greater value. Toys were donated to the United States Marine Corps Toys for Tots program and a domestic violence shelter for women and children. Many students would take advantage of this program near the end of the semester, because the university held back college transcripts, grades, and graduation for students with outstanding parking tickets. A great way for the public to pay off citations, and it was always enjoyable for me to come into the office to find our waiting area filled with toys.

Parking Meter Change for Change

Our Authority Parking Meter Change for Change program takes old parking meters and places them next to the garage elevators. Signage indicates that the money collected will be donated to an area charity. You would be surprised how much money in quarters you can collect for charity at only a few meters, usually around $500.

CHAPTER TWENTY-THREE

...AND LOWS

Physical Attacks on Staff

Luckily, I have never had an employee killed on the job, but that does not keep the public from verbally abusing or causing physical injury. There are several incidents that I remember well.

One started when a doctor was complaining about a parking fee. Our cashier got a manager on the phone and handed the phone over to the doctor. When he was told that he would indeed have to pay for parking, the doctor threw the phone and it hit the cashier in the head, causing bleeding and bruising. The doctor denied the incident, but it was all caught on camera. He was disciplined by his superiors and had to write an apology to the cashier. Sounds like grade school, but lucky for him, he was not fired.

I had a parking attendant have his foot run over. He and other personnel were blocking the garage entrance when it was full. I guess the driver thought "I am entering the garage. If you are in the way, too bad. I am getting into the garage, one way or another!" The police dealt with that incident.

Murder in a Garage

A fight that began in a nightclub next to one of our garages ended in the garage elevator lobby, where an individual was murdered. After the obvious chaos from this situation, a memorial was started with signs and candles, on the site in front of the elevators within the garage.

There was a balance to be kept between respect for the deceased's memorial and the need for customers to use the garage and elevator. We coordinated with those involved to allow for a memorial service on the site over a weekend, when parking activity was not as busy, and then respectfully removed the memorial. I hope you never have to deal with such a tragic situation.

Death Threats

I received my first death threat over the phone from a phone number that was traceable outside the state. There was not much the police could do, but really, a death threat over a $15 parking ticket? Unfortunately, such threats are not uncommon; they are mostly directed toward staff.

RIP

If you work long enough, you deal with the death of employees. One that hit me hardest was a man I had worked with for many years, a valued parking manager. He always had a smile on his face, was loyal and always protected my best interest. He was in his mid-thirties with three young children. It was a typical Friday and at the end of the day, he said, "See you boss, have a great weekend." Well, he died in a car accident over that weekend. It rocked me then and it still weighs on me twenty-five years later. From that day forward, I am always cognizant to appreciate the people around me. Continue to rest in peace, Mr. Brittingham.

Divorce

A doctor's wife was going through a divorce and claimed her husband was having an affair. Her lawyer subpoenaed his daily parking card access records to verify when he was arriving and leaving work. Those records told a different story than the doctor had told his wife and helped her obtain a divorce rather quickly.

Fights over Parking Spots

"Wild Parking Spot Brawl in NYC Turns into Violent Road Rage Crash"

How often do we read about fights, sometimes resulting in death, serious injury, or property damage, over a parking space? Such altercations often occur in a city where street parking is scarce, in a mall lot during the busy Christmas season, or after someone has dug their car out of two feet of snow, subsequently feels ownership of the spot and places a chair or object down to reserve the space. No individual owns the public streets. A parking disagreement is certainly not worth injury or death.

Smear Campaign

I have overseen many formal bids for work at the organizations I have run over the years. But the award for "Nastiest Vendor" goes to a business that would simply not accept the fact that they did not win a bid for services. I have always communicated afterwards with vendors who lose bids to let them know why they did not get the business. It is usually a personal call, which they at least say they appreciate receiving from me. I am open and honest in my assessment. Some appreciate it, while others do not.

The nastiest vendor was so angry at losing the bid that he kept calling and harassing anyone he could talk to in our organization until the point where no one would accept his call. He won the award, however, by taking his harassment a step further. He had his attorney send letters attacking my integrity to all board members, all city council members, and the mayor. Nothing came about as a result of sending these letters. The only outcome was to make him, and his company, look like the sore losers they happen to be.

When I was at a conference several months later, I avoided all their employees. I had a board of director position in the organization I was serving on, and I was up on stage giving out awards to my peers. A friend of mine told me that he was seated at their table, and when they saw me on stage, they realized I was well connected in the industry.

They spent the remainder of the week trying to chase me down to apologize, finally cornering me outside the exhibit hall on the streets and asking what they needed to do to make amends. I stated that they must send a retraction letter to everyone in my city they had sent letters to. They did. Unfortunately, they did not learn their lesson; several peers have called me since that time to state they had done the same scurrilous things to them. For obvious reasons I cannot print the name and company here. I can only hope bad karma finds its way to them one day.

When I Knew it Was Over

I had spent almost eight years building a parking program at a university. Due to cost cutting measures, my department was split into three other departments. When I asked the senior vice president why they were doing this to a department that generated over $12 million for the university, his response was, "We're in the education business, not the parking business." And then I told him, "I am in the parking business." It was my "Ah ha" moment and after that brief conversation I started looking for a new job.

Nasty Customers

I have had many employees over the years quit because they could not handle the abuse from customer interactions. Dealing with angry, nasty, crazy customers falls into the 10% of the 80-10-10 rule discussed earlier in the book. I empathize that no one ever wants to get a parking ticket for any reason. This is their money wasted that could be used to pay bills, buy dinner out or just about anything else. But hate can run deep at times as discussed in the next several anecdotes.

An individual posted a social media review that she does not like the parking authority. Okay, but she takes it a step further and must point out at the time that I did not live in town. No idea how she knew. Maybe a friend or enemy told a friend. The following is an excerpt from the post:

"The Parking Authority is legitimately one of the most corrupt businesses. The guy who runs it supposedly doesn't even live in the area. And the people who work there are cogs in a machine who are more than happy to get paid to take advantage of hard-working people."

This one was not too bad, but the following will be worse.

WARNING: I debated whether to include photos of the exact emails and personal checks in this part of the book to emphasis and create shock value of how mean people can be when communicating with a parking authority. After input from my editor, and in talking with family and friends, I decided to omit specific documents, but would put in verbatim what was written and received in my office. As my editor told me, these are not in the true tone of the overall book, and I agree, but I thought it was important to share this disturbing side of the business and the mental abuse that sometimes occurs.

Personal checks for payment of parking tickets often have a "Memo" or "For" line on the front bottom left hand corner to write a comment. Some of the nastier comments we have received say,

- "Choke on it"

- "F*cking Parking Ticket"

- and of course *"F*ck You".*

We deposit the checks and happily take their money.

This email was particularly terrible and hateful:

*Mike H*nt*

*1875 F*ck You Blvd*

Lazy Town, Pennsylvania 17804

*"You're all f*gs. F*ck you and your bullsh*t tickets for street cleaning"*

This email line was strange but at least somewhat creative:

- "Eat sh*t you overpaid kingdom of gloom monkeys."

We Are the Devil!

- Copies of this blurry photograph were placed on multi-space kiosks in the city. It spooked many of my employees and the public that saw it. It *is* disturbing, but I found it bizarrely creative in that someone would go to all that trouble to show dissatisfaction with the parking authority.

Awkward Envelope

I decided this one wasn't too bad to show. Funny in a five-year old way.

Cheaters Email

One of the more unique excuses. Is it too much information to tell the parking authority your intimate relationship issues as justification to get a ticket dismissed? I have kept the original wording.

"I would like to dispute two tickets. I just found out about these tickets. My boyfriend has been cheating and dropping me off to work and then going to see the other girl. Any way if I prove I was working then to get the tickets into his name? I don't think I should have to pay for his mistakes when I'm already paying with a broken heart....thanks."

Poo Parking

I have talked earlier about the challenges dealing with the homeless and those with mental health issues. This is spray painted on a garage I am looking to acquire. I have been warned.

CHAPTER TWENTY-FOUR

THE LIGHTER SIDE OF PARKING

Seinfeld

I could not write a book about the quirky world of parking without paying proper homage to the television show, Seinfeld. In episodes throughout the years, parking was a vital part of the storyline. Several of the more famous episodes include:

- *"The Parking Garage"* used a parking garage setting for the entire episode.

- *"The Parking Space"* explored the merits of backing-in versus pulling-in to a street space and who should have priority when both drivers arrive at the same time.

- *"The Smelly Car"* was especially poignant and my favorite since I had my valet company at that time. Jerry Seinfeld had bought a new BMW and had the car valet parked. When he got the car back, it reeked from body odor from the valet. Even after many attempts to clean the car, he could not get rid of the smell. He eventually left the car to be stolen, and even the thieves did not want the smelly vehicle.

In a recent interview, Seinfeld said you know you have made it in the entertainment business when you can park your (fancy) car in front of a New York City restaurant or comedy club and you don't have to worry about paying the parking ticket; as long as the car is not towed!

The Best Recruitment Trip Ever

Years ago, I applied for a vice president position overseeing parking, transportation, and other auxiliary services at a major university as I sought career advancement. It was always a challenge to be promoted within your own university. You do a great job for years, but you are always seen as the parking guy or gal. You may get a cursory promotion in title, maybe from director to executive director, but not real growth and income opportunity.

There have been some recent success stories with my peers, which is great. But for me, when I was trying to move up in the world, I would scan jobs looking for vice president level positions, regardless of the location.

I was excited to be offered an interview for a vice president position. The first interview went great and a second interview was requested. For the second interview, the university said I could bring my family and they would handle all the arrangements. To my surprise, the trip started with a first-class flight. We were then picked up from the airport in a limousine. The limo driver holding a sign with our name on it was cool to my young family not used to this level of special treatment. Then off to overnight accommodations at the Ritz Carlton. At the Ritz Carlton, we were greeted upon entering our room with a gift basket filled with university swag; hats, shirts, and umbrellas; I guess it rains there a lot! Plus, candy and two huge cookies with my two little boys' names on them. Did they mix me up with a five-star All-American football recruit, top notch doctor or professor? I guess they wanted to make a great impression on my family and wanted me to take the job. I just wouldn't dare tell anyone at the university my boys ate all the candy that night and one of them vomited all over the once nice Ritz Carlton bedding. The next day my wife and kids spent the day as tourists while I had a long day in interviews. In case you haven't noticed yet from a previous story, universities like long full day interviews with many stakeholders. Although the day was grueling, I thought it went well. My last interview of the day was with their executive vice president, in what would be the most surreal negotiation of my life. He says to me, "we want to offer you the director of parking position." I was perplexed that I was not getting the vice president position. But he put on a full court press and continued, "I know you are the best at what you do, so name your price." Name my price? The movie Austin Powers, and the character Dr. Evil starts running through my head as I am thinking 'one million dollars' with my pinkie on the corner of my mouth. But that was not the full extent of the offer. Moving expenses, OK. Free tuition for my kids, OK. Six months free living expense, OK. Five figure bonus, OK. And a great salary. I was on an immense high as I contemplated this move in my life. In the end, I did not feel it was worth uprooting my family for a position I felt was a lateral move and would not provide enough job satisfaction. Additionally, contemplating a move to a new university in a far-away city and how easily could a lifetime east coast guy adapt. Call me crazy, but never just chase the money. Make sure the job will be fulfilling so that you do not regret the move a year later. But I must admit, being treated like a superstar recruit was a blast.

Wedding Bells

It is wonderful to bring together employees or friends that end up getting married. My first match was several years after college. I introduced my college roommate to my friend from student government. They never interacted in college but met while both were working for my valet parking company. They are still together after 30 years.

Next, I introduced a good friend to a restaurant owner's radio marketing exec where my company handled valet parking. They have also been married for 30 years and owe it all to me!

Just as fulfilling is having two parking attendants meet through work and get married. I have lost touch after all these years, but I know they have kids. Hopefully little parking attendants in training.

Cohenisms

Scattered within the book are many sayings I have acquired and used over the years. Here are a couple my staff reminded me that I use on occasion.

"I See the Train Coming" means, based on past experiences, there is a high probability I know the outcome of a decision and it may not be a very good decision or outcome. Do not just stand there if you are on the train tracks and let the train hit you. Get out of the way! If possible, try to change things before you are affected by someone else's bad decision. When someone asks me, "How do you usually make the right decision?" I tell them it is from years of experience and getting hit by the train several times. Growing old does have some advantages.

"It is Always a Full Moon at the Parking Authority" Often, when a crazy incident occurs, I always swear there is a full moon on that day. Do you use the same line? I bet you do.

Lights, Camera, Action!

My programs have hosted many events, photo shoots and music videos over the years. The coolest of the engagements was while I was at the hospital. We hosted the movie shoot for a Morgan

Freeman film called *Along Came a Spider*. I know this is commonplace in California and other movie hot spots, but for us it was exciting. It was a decent movie and the producers paid a nice fee for the use of a parking garage for a couple days of shooting their scenes at night.

Ice Breaker

One of my favorite meeting "ice breaker" stories is to tell how I played hooky from high school with a friend and headed down to the Philadelphia Art Museum area to be extras in the movie *Rocky II*. We followed Sylvester Stallone on his run up the Benjamin Franklin Parkway and up the Art Museum steps along with hundreds of other kids. If you do not blink, you may see my head in the crowd.

The National Enquirer

Working at a world class hospital lent itself to seeing famous people arriving at the hospital for treatment for medical issues. I can tell you we arranged transportation and parking for some of the most notable A-list celebrities in the world. Of course, we were sworn to secrecy and could not tell anyone these celebrities were at the hospital and why they were admitted. If I wanted to make a lot of money, I could have called *The National Enquirer*. The tabloid would have had some really good front page stories over the years. I would never do such a thing, but the stories I could tell...

Lizard Lady

Of course, you can bring your lizard into my office when paying your parking ticket! Look closely, this is a bearded dragon, and they are friendly, but regardless, this is one of the stranger pets that has watched its owner handle a parking transaction. I used to have several bearded dragons, so I was not afraid of it or her!

The ABC's of Parking

Just a fun exercise. Can you think of any better ones? Let me know!

- Architecture

- Budgets

- Cashless Transactions

- Development

- Enforcement
- Free Parking
- Garages
- Helix
- Integrity
- Judicial Process
- Kiosks
- Leadership
- Meters
- Networking
- Operations
- Public Relations
- Question, Persuade and Refer (Suicide Mitigation Training)
- Revenue Control
- Spaces
- Technology
- Uses for Garages and Lots
- Valet
- Welcoming
- Xcited About ...
- You are a Parking Professional
- Zero Tolerance for Theft

The Twelve Days of Free Holiday Parking

A staff member wrote the following lyric to coincide with the free meter parking days that we provide on the streets around Christmas. There is also a corresponding video which I would rather not share and be embarrassed by!

Feel free to sing along to the tune of "The 12 Days of Christmas" and with apologies to Frederic Austin.

On the 1st day of free parking, I went downtown to see

The holiday decorations and the tree.

On the 2nd day of free parking, I checked out what's on stage

I got tickets for the play that's all the rage.

On the 3rd day of free parking, to Central Market I did go

To buy the stuff to make my cookie dough.

On the 4th day of free parking, I was hungry as can be

I found a restaurant downtown for me.

On the 5th day of free parking, I thought again, it's free!

Free on-street parking!

On the 6th day of free parking, I needed desperately

Some Yuletide for me and presents for my friends and family.

On the 7th day of free parking, I checked on my cell phone

There was no enforcement in this zone!

On the 8th day of free parking, I was running out of steam

So, I found a shop and cuppa coffee with cream.

On the 9th day of free parking, my family and me

Went downtown to see Santa by the tree.

On the 10th day of free parking, I just needed some time

To walk around, relax and unwind.

On the 11th day of free parking, my heart was full of cheer

I looked around and found no Scrooges here!

On the 12th day of free parking, I went downtown with glee

To return the gifts that were not right for me.

Eight Crazy Nights

Not to be outdone, I have created a list of what I wish for in parking operations. With only *"Eight Crazy Nights"*, as coined by Adam Sandler, these coincide with Hanukkah.

- On the first night, no more customer complaints about paying for parking and citations.

- On the second night, no more free parking, ever.

- On the third night, customers who always welcome the use of new technology.

- On the fourth night, garages that never need structural repairs.

- On the fifth night, staff that always smile and are never dishonest.

- On the sixth night, money to upgrade to all the latest technology.

- On the seventh night, bosses that always value parking professionals.

- And on the eighth crazy night, vacation without an emergency call or email!

"White Stuff"

Snow and parking do not mix well, just like oil and vinegar, or in this case salt and water. You can spend hundreds of thousands of dollars each year on snow removal. Snow removal can wreak havoc on the best of budgets. A yearly variable in our budget is predicting how much money will be needed for snow removal. We typically budget on a three year average. Being in the Northeast, in some years we get no snow and in other years we get lots. Invariably, as soon as you cut back snow removal expenses from the budget, you get dumped upon. So, in heavy areas of the country, garages are designed to handle easier snow removal. I saw this snow ramp on a recent visit to Appleton, Wisconsin, near Lambeau Field (home of the Green Bay Packers).

Museums

The Henry Ford Museum in Dearborn, Michigan, has a section on parking meters. The exhibit has a sign that says "Controlling the Chaos". It is great that the museum recognizes that parking meters were put in place to bring civility to the streets. The sign reads:

"By the 1920s, automobile parking on city streets was out of control. Cities tried everything. They widened streets. They prohibited parking by fire hydrants and intersections. They marked out parking spaces. Finally, the parking meter proved workable and enforceable. It relieved traffic congestion and increased revenue for governments. Tickets and fines forced motorists to accept the meters."

The National Building Museum in Washington, D.C., has also had exhibits related to parking. The university at the time donated an old parking gate for the exhibit.

The Beautification of Parking Garages

We have come a long way in designing parking garages that can double as works of art. The first American city to fully embrace art as part of parking garages is Santa Monica, California. Why did I visit? Of course, to see the parking garages!. The Santa Monica Pier is nice as well. These are two of the many cool structures through-out the city.

Below is of one of our award-winning garages that blends the parking garage into the surrounding buildings.

One of my favorite quirky garages that a friend owned. It is the Rolls Royce Garage in Chicago, Illinois. It is in the style of art deco.

Vertical Greenhouse

There was a proposed for-profit venture to build a Green Urban Farm greenhouse along a small strip of land next to our garage for growing and harvesting vegetables. It was modeled after the first one, built in Jackson Hole, Wyoming, but ours has not come to fruition yet.

Pop-Up Parks

At certain times of the year, notably on Park(ing) Day, parking spaces throughout the country are converted into creative uses. Here are some from our city.

Garage Murals

Here are beautiful murals painted at our garages. The artist is shown with her work.

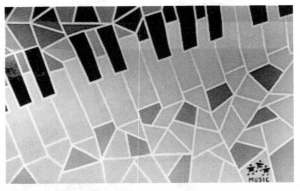

C H A P T E R T W E N T Y - F I V E

PARKING TCHOTCHKES

Tchotchkes (pronounced ChaCh-keys) is a Yiddish word that describes a trinket or smallish collectible. Over the course of my 40-year career, I have collected many and have received other items as gifts. Here are some.

Every parking professional who has been in the business for a while has the obligatory parking meter bank. These are old parking meters turned into personal banks. A place to deposit your coins, but not coins from where you work!

Movies about Parking

There are few movies about parking but grab some popcorn and watch:

The Delicate Art of Parking and

The Parking Lot Movie

Both are on DVD. You may perhaps find them for sale on the internet.

Board Games

There are at least two board games for the parking aficionado:

Free Parking and

Park and Shop

I have both, but I confess I have never played them.

The Parking Lot Game is an old math game from the 1950s that I have in my collection.

The Beatles made famous Lovely Rita Meter Maid. There is her figurine.

Odd Ball Items

How about a quilt? (Courtesy of my mother-in-law.) It hangs behind my desk.

A meter maid voodoo doll. From New Orleans, of course. By the way, it has not worked - yet.

Computer Mouse Pad
A nice gift from my deputy. Thanks Susan.

Vinyl Record

Good music? Let me know if you ever listened to this 1976 album by Stu Daye called *Free Parking*.

Greeting Card

Very corny.

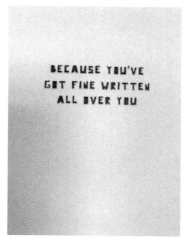

T-Shirts

Wildly creative.

I like the shirt, but I would not wear it in public without crazy reactions!

Art

Print commissioned by a parking supplier.

Bought from a street vendor in New York City.

An artist's view and rendering of one of our garages.

Neon at its best.

Magazine Cover

An iconic parking sign and sculpture across from Philadelphia City Hall became my winning Parking Photo of the Year and was put on the cover of our trade publication. It is located across from Philadelphia City Hall.

Figurines
Salt and Pepper, anyone?

Ballet (or is it valet?) parking, by Will Bullas.

Beach parking would be very nice, especially over long bitter winters.

License Plates

These are license plates I have had on my various cars throughout the years. In hindsight, it may not have been the best idea to stand out so much and say, "Here's the parking guys car." I never did use this license plate frame on my cars, but I love the motto.

If you don't have a vanity plate, you can always use this license plate frame.

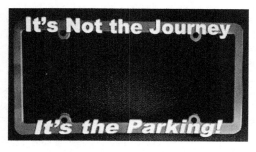

Ties

I usually wear a special tie for special parking events, so which one do you prefer?

 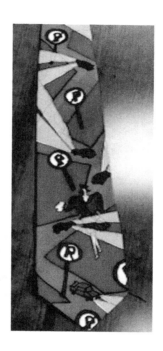

Metal Art

Is it No Parking for the person or vehicle or both?

A tow truck in front of the Unites States capitol! How could I not pass up this work of art?

The perfect business card holder.

Comics

Creative marketing, comic book style.

What could make a kid happier than a parking activity book?

Parking has been a problem for as long as vehicles have been around. This is a great photo from New York City in front of the Famous Delicatessen.

PARKING HAS ALWAYS BEEN
A PROBLEM.

An example of "what is old is new again". As discussed in my trip to Italy, here is an automated elevator garage from New York City in 1920. Automated parking garages in the 21st century take on all shapes and sizes (above and below ground) as I learned when visiting parking garages in Europe one summer.

Elevator parking lot in New York, 1920

Signs

An entire book could be dedicated to all the crazy parking signs in the world. Here is one to remind you that all signs are not created equal!

In Lancaster, Pennsylvania, home of the Amish, a shovel and wheel-barrow along with a "Horse and Buggy Parking Only" sign is not unusual.

EPILOGUE

The End of the Road

As a little boy, I always dreamed of being a baseball player. In my younger years, I was an avid collector of baseball cards (even bought my first house from the sale of some of my collection) and dreamed my own autograph could also be valuable one day.

Well, the value in my signature now comes every Friday when I sign authority checks to pay the bills. Now, since I have written a book, I hope friends and peers ask for a signed copy. I will be more than happy to oblige! Making my autograph dreams come true at this point in my life! Thank you!

In the end, no matter what profession we choose, we should always put family first. Isn't that what matters most? I have also been blessed to find a quirky profession that I have enjoyed and embraced for four decades. Most folks cannot wait to retire, but I cannot wait to get to work and see what new challenges and new stories arise. Call me masochistic about work if you want. But family is always top priority.

The only thing I ever wanted from my kids for holidays, birthdays, and Father's Days were homemade cards. Below are two of my favorites, one each from their younger years. Now that my sons are in their twenties, they are not enthused about making cards anymore and would rather buy me a gift. Therefore, I suggest that you ask for these gems while the kids are young!

In closing, I am humbled that you have taken the time to read my book. Feel free to email, call, or visit my website at ljcohen-consulting.com to let me know what you thought of the book, what I should have included, where I was totally wrong, and if you have any general questions about the parking business, I will try to answer them. And please leave a review on the site you purchased the book, it is motivation to start working on a revised version or a new book with new stories to tell since there are always more every day!

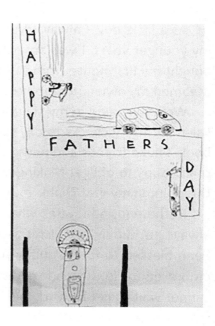

Made in the USA
Middletown, DE
22 May 2021

39737895R00116